Alex & Sandra Leggatt

CARPENTRY
FOR THE HOME

B T Batsford Ltd London

To all our friends, for their help — thanks

Printed in Great Britain by
The Anchor Press, Tiptree, Essex
for the publishers B T Batsford Ltd
4 Fitzhardinge Street, London W1H 0AH

CONTENTS

FOREWORD

The home carpenter is a person who goes by results. He or she enjoys making things to enhance the home or please the children. The methods used here are not always 'correct' in terms of traditional carpentry, but in our experience, using modern glues and materials, they work.

All the projects given here, and the simple techniques required, are set out in step-by-step fashion, thus assuring success in small or large items for even the most inexperienced worker.

With a very small and inexpensive tool-kit, comprising only five purchased tools, it is possible to work through this book from beginning to end. Initial outlay therefore is not a major problem. If you need it, make it!

MEASUREMENTS

All the measurements in this book are given in metric and imperial units. The conversion factor is usually understood to be 25.4 mm = 1 inch, or 10 mm = $\frac{3}{8}$ inch. If this conversion is followed too strictly it can lead to some very awkward numbers, so rather than use direct conversions in each case, the projects have been worked out separately in each system. While working through the instructions, use the system with which you feel the most comfortable, and do not change from one system to the other within the course of a project.

When buying materials, ask the timber merchant for advice on the exact sizes required for the work involved. Most merchants are able to supply planed timber in the exact metric sizes requested. Rough timber however comes in standard sizes from the sawmill, known as the nominal size (abbreviated to nom throughout the text). Working in inches, a piece of timber '4 x 1 in' is planed down to approximately $3\frac{7}{8}$ x $\frac{7}{8}$ inches section, yet sold as '4 x 1 in' nominal size.

Where three measurements are given for a particular item, they are given in the following order throughout the book: width x thickness (i.e. the cross section) x length.

TOOLS

In general, it is sound advice to buy the best tools you can afford. It is on this point that the projects in this book offer a great advantage, since only five tools need be purchased to cover all the requirements. A good tool bought from a reputable dealer may cost more than a lower quality item, but could represent a life-time investment.

Make the bench-hook described here before beginning any of the projects, and make the adjustable cramp when the need arises.

Saws

The panel saw is a good general-purpose saw. The one shown here is coated with a modern PTFE-based material to help prevent the saw from jamming in the wood. (PTFE = poly-tetra-fluoro-ethylene.)

The tenon saw is normally used for accurate cabinetwork. Because of its stiff back strut, however, it cannot cut deeper than about 70 mm (3 in).

Screwdriver

Buy a screwdriver with a well-rounded, comfortable handle such as the one shown on the left in the illustration. The screwdriver on the right would be likely to blister the palm of an unaccustomed hand after only a few minutes serious use. Ask the dealer for a screwdriver suitable for No. 6 and No. 8 screw heads.

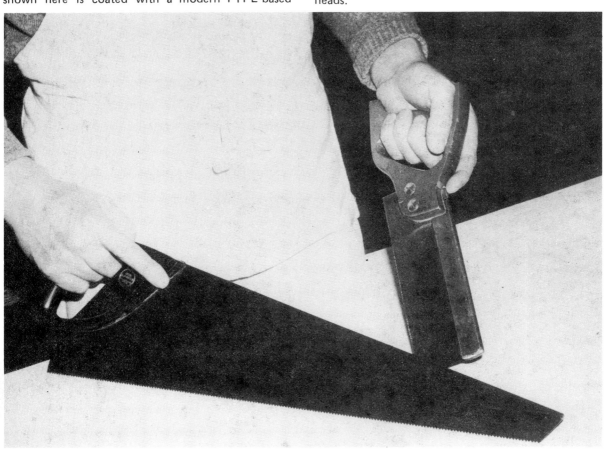

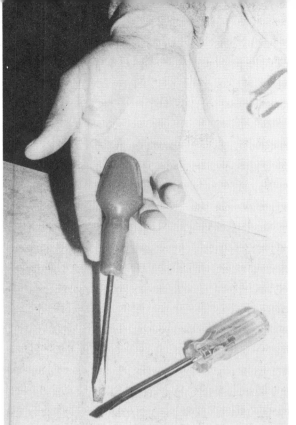

1 *Opposite Left* panel saw; *right* tenon saw

2 *Left* The screwdriver on the right is unsuitable for carpentry; the one on the left has a well-rounded, comfortable handle

3 *Below Left* claw hammer; *right* Warrington hammer and nail-extracting pliers

Hammer

Do not buy a hammer which is too heavy. You must be able to use it when holding the shaft at the correct hand position. Buy either a claw hammer or the more lightweight Warrington hammer plus a pair of nail-extracting pliers.

Surform

These tools come in many variations. Perhaps the best initial buy is the one shown in the left of the illustration. It is shown here as a plane, but the handle can be easily reversed to lie parallel to the body giving a tool with the same handling characteristics as a file; it is called a 'planer/file' (see page 10).

A Surform with a blunt blade is an inefficient tool, so buy a few spare blades at the time of purchase.

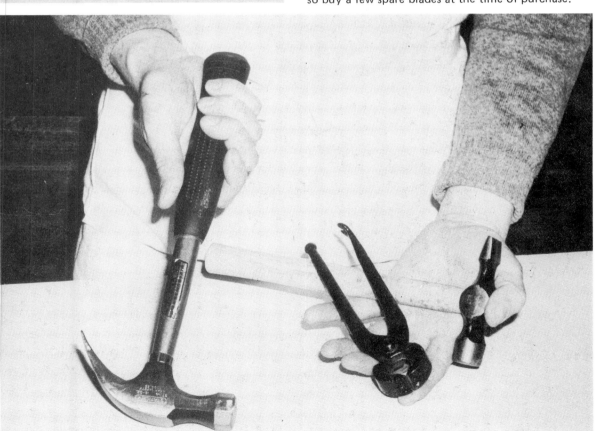

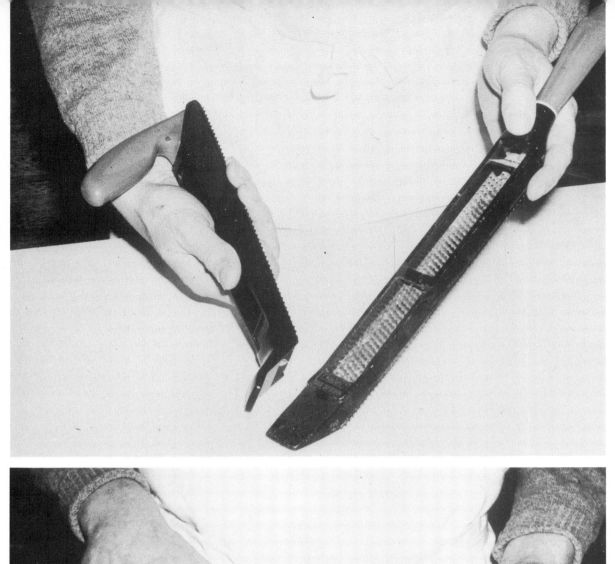

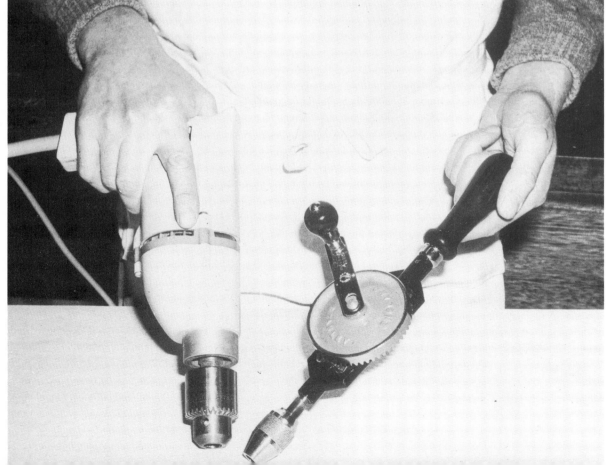

Drill

Drills are available in both electric and hand-driven versions. Do not shun the hand drill as being old-fashioned — with a little practice it becomes an efficient tool, safe and reliable.

Twist drill bits will be required, and these can be bought in sets, but if buying them separately start off with the following diameters: 2.5 mm ($\frac{3}{32}$ in), 3.5 mm ($\frac{1}{8}$ in), 4.5 mm ($\frac{3}{16}$ in) and 9.5 mm ($\frac{3}{8}$ in). If the drill chuck will not expand to a size suitable for the 9.5 mm ($\frac{3}{8}$ in) drill bit, buy the largest bit that the drill will take.

Measuring tape

A good quality dressmaker's tape will suffice, but a 2 metre (6 feet) steel tape is more durable and easier to use.

Square

The 90° or right angle is most important in carpentry, but it is not necessary to buy a proper carpenter's try-square immediately if expense is a problem. Ask your materials supplier for a piece of thin plywood about 300 mm (12 in) square which has been cut on a power saw. The corners of this should be 90° (if you explain to the dealer why you need it he may be only too please to help).

Sanding block

This can be a device into which abrasive paper is clipped, but is more likely to be block of cork which can be comfortably hand-held, around which the abrasive paper can be wrapped. A piece of wood approximately 100 x 60 mm (4 x $2\frac{1}{2}$ in) and 25 mm (1 in) thick makes a good substitute.

Bench hook

The bench hook is an essential piece of equipment for most of the projects in this book, so make it before proceeding.

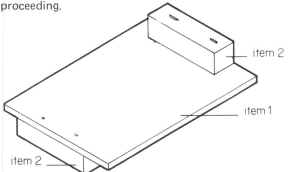

item 2

item 1

item 2

Materials

Item no.	Description	Quantity
1	plywood or chipboard (particle board) 150 x 9 (minimum) x 200 mm (6 x $\frac{3}{8}$ (minimum) x 8 in)	1
2	pine or hardwood 40 x 20 x 100 mm (2 x 1 nom x 4 in)	2
3	oval brad nails 35 mm ($1\frac{1}{2}$ in)	4
4	PVA woodworker's adhesive	

Method

1 Mark the position of one of the short lengths (item 2) on the piece of board (item 1) and hammer two oval brad nails into this area until the nail tips just protrude through the board (Figure 2).

2 Apply glue liberally to the wider face of item 2 and place this on a piece of waste wood. Position the board as indicated and drive home the nails. If the nails protrude, clench them over in the direction of the grain (Figure 3).

3 Repeat for the second item 2. Wipe off the excess glue with a damp cloth, then leave until the glue has set.

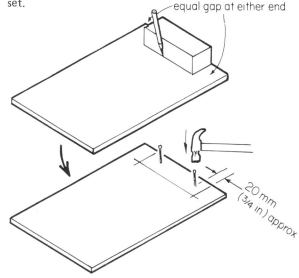

equal gap at either end

20 mm (3/4 in) approx

Figure 1 *Left* Assembling items 1 and 2

Figure 2 *Above* Hammering two oval brad nails into the board

4 *Opposite above* The Surform is on the left; the 'Planer/File' is the best initial buy

5 *Opposite below Left* electric power drill; *right* hand drill

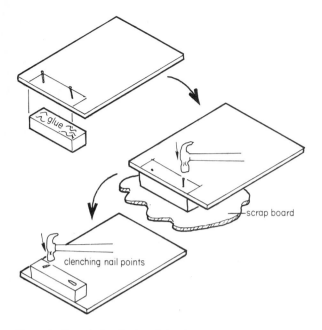

Figure 3 Completing the bench hook

Cramp

The specialist cramps called 'sash cramps' are really beyond the scope of all but the very keenest home carpenters. The cramp shown here is an effective alternative and can be made very simply and cheaply.

It is the only cramping device which will be required for any of the projects in this book, and it may not be required at all for the particular items which you may intend to tackle.

Materials

Item no.	Description	Quantity
1	hardwood 45 x 45 x 200 mm (2 x 2 x 8 in)	3
2	chipboard (particle board)/ plywood/blockboard 200 mm x 25 mm x 1 m (8 in x 1 in x $3\frac{1}{2}$ ft)	1
3	crosshead screws and nuts 6 mm diameter x 120 mm long ($\frac{1}{4}$ in diameter x 5 in long)	2
4	bolts with nuts 6 mm diameter x 80 mm long ($\frac{1}{4}$ in diameter x $3\frac{1}{2}$ in long)	4

Method

1 The fixed block (item 1) should be held in position against the edge of the board (item 2). An extra pair of hands would be helpful at this stage to hold the block with the edges marked X flush, while the vertical bolt holes are drilled. These should be 6 mm ($\frac{1}{4}$ in) in diameter and 25 mm (1 in) from the outside edges as shown in Figure 5. After the blocks have been permanently bolted in position the adjusting screw holes (labelled B in Figure 5) are drilled. These should be 6 mm ($\frac{1}{4}$ in) diameter.

2 The adjustable block is now drilled through 6 mm ($\frac{1}{4}$ in) diameter, 25 mm (1 in) in from either end, and to make sure that it is never fixed in position the wrong way round, which could result in non-parallel cramping faces, 'cramping face' or something to that

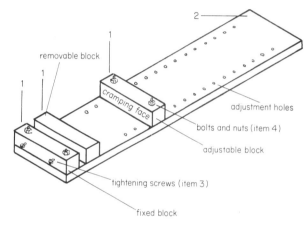

Figure 4 Positioning the blocks

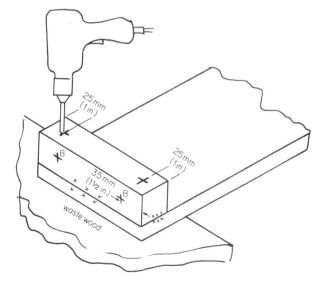

Figure 5 Drilling the bolt holes

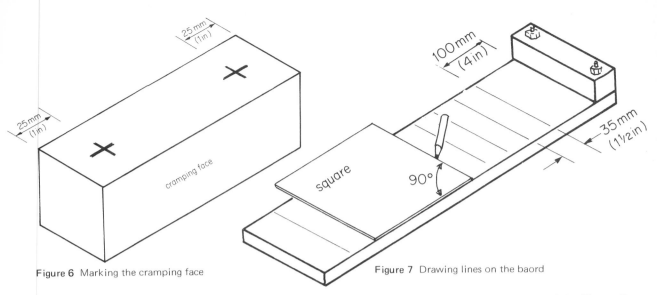

Figure 6 Marking the cramping face

Figure 7 Drawing lines on the baord

effect should be written on the block as indicated in Figure 6.

3 Starting about 100 mm (4 in) from the fixed block, draw lines on the board, 35 mm ($1\frac{1}{2}$ in) apart (Figure 7). Ensure that each line is at 90° to the edge by using your square (see Tools, page 11).

Hold the edge of the adjustable block against each of these lines in turn, and drill through the existing 6 mm ($\frac{1}{4}$ in) diameter holes in the block right through the baseboard (Figure 8). Again an extra pair of hands may be useful.

4 The use of the cramp is illustrated in Figure 9. Consider item *A* is to be cramped to item *B*. First, retract the tightening screw(s) until the nut is at the end of the screw. The adjustable block is bolted into position, so that the initial gap is as small as it can be while still allowing the cramped items *A* and *B* to sit in place.

The base of the cramp should be lined with paper if glue is being used, to prevent sticking.

The job is then placed in position and the screw(s) tightened (Figure 10).

If you find that the ends of the tightening screws are seriously damaging the removable block, you could use a strip of metal, for the screws to bear against.

Figure 8 Drilling holes into the baseboard

Figure 9 The cramp in use

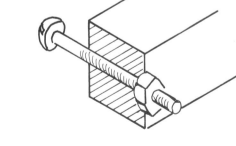

Figure 10 *Above* Sectional detail of the tightening screw

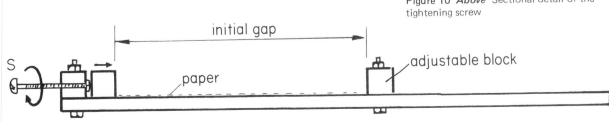

13

TECHNIQUES

Nailing

Watch any carpenter at work and you will see that he always holds his hammer at the end of the shaft. This is partly so that a greater striking force can be achieved, but it also has the effect of discouraging nails from their infuriating habit of bending each time they are struck.

Figure 11 shows (above) that the correctly held hammer is more likely to hit the nail square on the head. The twisting action of the wrist when the hammer is wrongly held results in an incorrect, glancing blow (Figure 11, below).

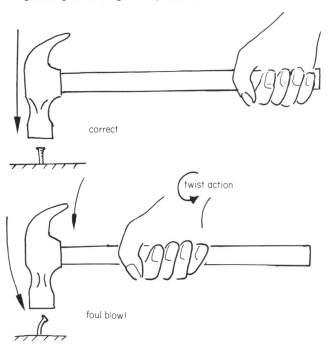

Figure 11 Holding the hammer (above) correctly and (below) incorrectly

Dovetail nailing

Nails are often used to hold two surfaces together until glue sets. The nails do this job best if they are hammered in, in pairs, at opposing angles (Figure 12). To do this, it is easier if you move yourself or the job

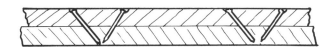

Figure 12 Dovetailed nails

so that you are always hammering downwards and towards yourself (Figure 13).

Nail-punching

This involves punching the head of the nail about 2 mm ($\frac{1}{16}-\frac{1}{8}$ in) below the surface using either a proper nail-punch or a 100 mm (4 in) wire-nail adapted by flattening its tip with a hammer (Figure 14). The punching is carried out as shown in Figure 15.

The punched hole can be filled with a stiff mixture of dust and glue or with a suitable woodfiller matched as closely as possible to the colour of the wood being filled.

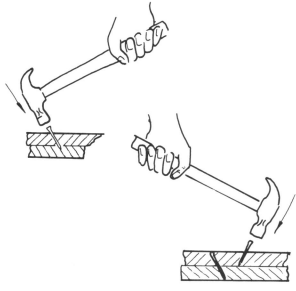

Figure 13 Changing position to hammer in each nail

14

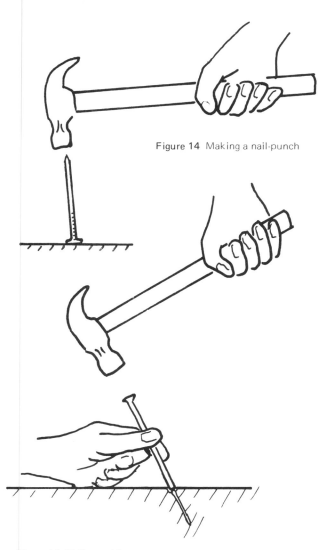

Figure 14 Making a nail-punch

Figure 15 Nail-punching

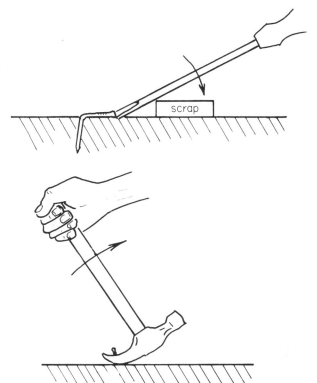

Figure 16 Prising out a bent nail

Nail extraction

Even experts make the occasional foul blow, result-ing in a nail so badly bent that it must be removed.

If the head of the nail is embedded in the surface, it should first be raised by prising it up with the tip of a screwdriver (Figure 16). A piece of scrap wood, used as shown, reduces the possibility of further surface damage being inflicted with the screwdriver.

Once the head of the nail has been prised up the claw of the hammer can be hooked under the nail head, and the nail can be removed by gently pulling.

Normally a second nail could then be hammered into the same spot. This is not possible, however, if the nail bent because its path was obstructed by a screw or some other metal object.

Screwdriving

Until you get the knack of using a screwdriver (make no mistake – it is not easy) the following rules help a great deal.

(a) Firstly always treat screwdriving as a two-handed job using the hand which is not on the handle to steady the screwdriver blade just above the tip, and push firmly downwards each time you twist (Figure 17).

(b) Make sure that the screwdriver blade is in line with the screw (Figure 18). Failure to do this is with-out a doubt the most likely error, and the cause of damaged screw heads.

When screwing softwood to softwood (as is the case with most projects in this book) two useful if some-what unconventional methods may be used.

Half hammer – half screw

A clearance hole, equal to the diameter of the screw's shank should be drilled in the top piece of wood (Figure 19a). If a countersunk screw head is being used, this piece of wood should also be countersunk or a cup-washer should be used.

15

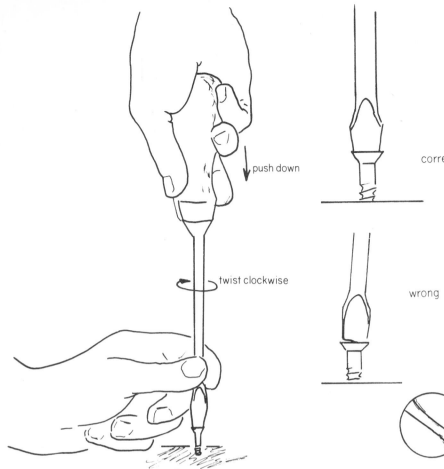

Figure 17 Using both hands to steady the screwdriver

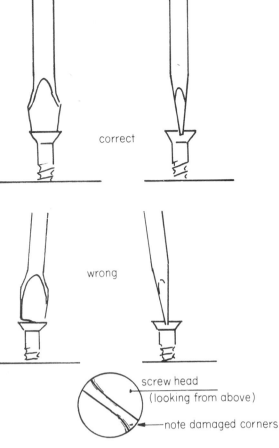

Figure 18 The screwdriver blade must be in line with the screw head

Figure 19 *Below* Half hammer, half screw

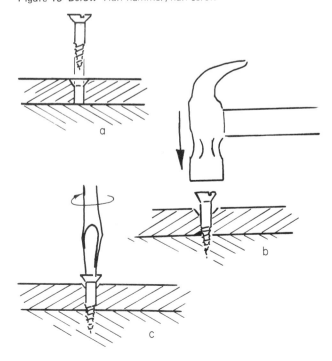

The pieces of wood should be brought together in the correct position, and the screw nail should be hammered halfway home (Figure 19*b*). This should be done with care as the head of the screw can be easily damaged. (If you find you are using excessive force with your hammer, try the method described below.)

The screw nail may now be driven fully home with the screwdriver (Figure 19*c*). Do not overtighten or you may strip the hole, rendering that screw almost ineffectual.

Pilot hole method

Here, as well as drilling a clearance hole in the top piece of wood, a smaller hole must be made in the lower piece to guide or pilot the screw.

The pilot hole may be drilled using a drill bit approximately half the diameter of the drill shank (Figure 20*a*). Alternatively (Figure 20*b*) a 35 mm (1½ in) round wire-nail or oval brad may be hammered in through the clearance hole and then extracted. (This nail size will do for No. 6 or No. 8

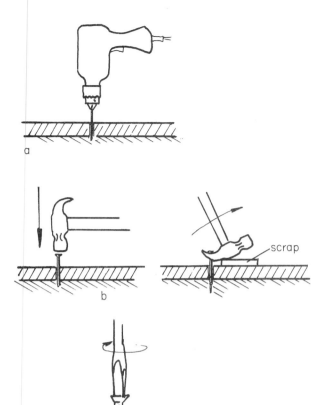

a

b

scrap

c clearance hole
pilot hole

Figure 20 The pilot-hole method

screws. For bigger or smaller screws use a correspondingly bigger or smaller wire-nail.)

The screw nail may then be screwed into the pilot hole (Figure 20c).

If the top piece of wood is fairly thin (e.g. plywood) you may, even after forming a pilot hole, have difficulty in starting the screw. If this is the case, then lightly hammer the screw a *little* way into the pilot hole, then finish off with the screwdriver.

At all times, if you find that the head of the screw is being damaged, remove that screw, discard it, and try again with a new one.

If you decide to use brass screws, either for their appearance or for their non-rusting properties, a little household soap smeared on the thread will make screwing them in much easier.

The following table below gives the normally acceptable pilot hole and clearance hole sizes for the three common sizes of nail used in this book.

Screw no.	6	8	10
pilot hole	2 mm ($\frac{3}{32}$ in)	3 mm ($\frac{1}{8}$ in)	3 mm ($\frac{1}{8}$ in)
clearance hole	3.5 mm ($\frac{1}{8}$ in)	4.5 mm ($\frac{3}{16}$ in)	4.5 mm ($\frac{3}{16}$ in)

Sawing

Most of the projects in this book require the use of a saw at some stage (Figure 21).

Regardless of the type of saw being used the grip is always similar: the saw should be held with three fingers and thumb, and the index finger pointing forward.

Position the saw on the desired line. Place your left thumb (if right-handed) against the flat of the saw, just above the teeth, to act as a guide. Draw the saw backwards three or four times to establish a

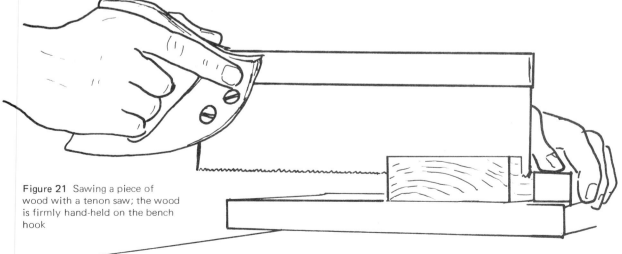

Figure 21 Sawing a piece of wood with a tenon saw; the wood is firmly hand-held on the bench hook

cutting line. Re-position the left thumb clear of the teeth and commence sawing. The essential point to remember is that you should concentrate on the sawing action and *not* on pushing the saw downwards. The saw teeth will do the cutting but only as long as they are kept moving.

If the saw jams, you have probably allowed the top edge of the blade to lie over either to the left or right.

Drilling

If you merely mark a drilling position in pencil and then start to drill, the drill tip will probably wander off position slightly before the tip bites. To avoid this, first mark the correct spot in pencil and hammer a nail into this position for about 3 mm ($\frac{1}{8}$ in). The mark left by the nail tip when the nail is removed will ensure that the hole is drilled accurately.

If you own a portable power drill, there are only two rules to remember. Firstly, keep the drill vertical both when drilling and when extracting the drill from the hole. Secondly, do not stop the motor when removing the bit from the finished hole. Switch off only when the drill bit is well clear of the hole.

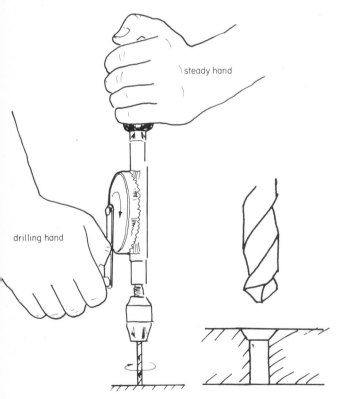

steady hand

drilling hand

Figure 22 *Left* Position of hands for drilling
Figure 23 *Right* Large drill bit used for countersinking

Failure to comply with these rules often results in a broken drill bit becoming firmly embedded.

With a hand drill (Figure 22) not only must these rules be obeyed (your drilling hand of course replaces the motor) but you must also avoid the temptation of pushing down heavily with your steadying hand. This does not speed the drilling action, but rather tends to cause jamming, with a possibility of the drill bit being broken.

Countersinking

This involves tapering the top edge of a screw clearance hole just enough to allow the head of a countersunk screw to be driven in flush with the surface (see Figure 23). You can do this either by using the largest available drill bit, or by using a special countersink bit.

Glues and gluing

The glues used by the modern carpenter can be broken down roughly into four groups as follows.

PVA
This is a thick, white liquid with a fairly short setting time (most joints can be handled within two hours) and good strength. It is not waterproof and should not be used on articles which are exposed continuously to an outside environment. It is the most popular of today's carpentry adhesives.

Urea formaldehyde
These glues are waterproof, and are most often used in the building of small boats. They are sold in two forms: 'one-shot', in which the powder is mixed with water and which will set within three hours, and 'two-shot', in which the powder is mixed with water and spread on one piece of wood while the mating piece is spread with a strong vinegar-scented, formic acid solution. This mixed resin will keep for a matter of weeks in an air-tight jar, so it can prove more economical than the 'one-shot' form although it is more difficult to use.

Impact adhesive
Normally these glues are used to fix large sheets of plastic laminate to boards (e.g. on kitchen work-tops).

Two-pack resin
This very strong, waterproof glue is sold in two separate tubes and is mixed just before use. A good general purpose adhesive, it will stick metal to wood, wood to plastic; and so on. It is, however, expensive if large quantities are required.

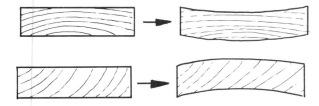

Figure 24 Warping in planks

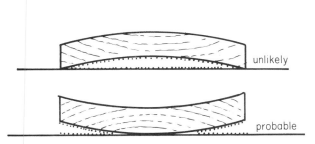

Figure 25 The effects of warping: the dotted line represents a broken glued joint

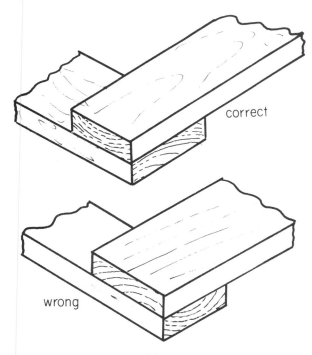

correct

wrong

Figure 26 Gluing a corner joint

Warping

For most jobs, when glue is used in conjunction with nails or screws, the only purpose of these fixings is to hold the joint together until the glue sets. Things become a little trickier, however, when a material having a relatively wide section is used, e.g. pine with a 95 mm x 20 mm (4 in x 1 in) section. It is necessary here to appreciate the difficulties that can be caused by the inevitable warping that will take place as the timber loses its natural moisture.

Warping occurs most readily in planks which have a pronounced bow pattern on the end grain of the timber. This bow is in fact a part of the tree's annual growth rings (Figure 24). If you imagine how these bows will straighten as the timber dries, then you will be able to predict the direction of the eventual warp.

If you are tearing a piece of cloth in half, you start from the edge, not the middle — it is easier that way. Likewise, a joint which is tending to tear itself free as a result of warping is much more likely to do so if it is the edges which warp first (see Figure 25). Here you can see that the joint which is unlikely to break has the bows pointing towards the glued surface. Figure 26 shows the right and wrong ways to glue a corner joint.

If the direction in which the bows point is not obvious, then it is probably safe to apply the glue to either face.

Rubbed joint

When a small, easily-handled piece of wood is being fixed to a larger piece, the use of the rubbing technique can minimise, and sometimes totally replace the use of other fixing devices such as nails, screws, or cramps.

A liberal smear of glue is applied to the joint area and the smaller block is rubbed backward and forward over the spot to expel air from the joint. It can then be slid to its final position where it is held by vacuum. Excess glue should be wiped off and the joint should be left until the glue has set.

Using this method, a length of beading about 300 mm (1 ft) long can be fixed into a corner using only two panel pins to stop it slipping from its final position (Figure 27).

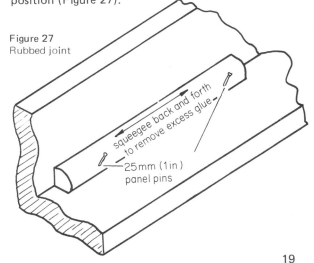

Figure 27
Rubbed joint

squeegee back and forth to remove excess glue

25 mm (1 in) panel pins

Keying

When gluing wood to melamine-coated chipboard (particle board) you must remember that the smooth plastic surface will not normally provide enough grip for the glue. The surface on which the glue is to be put must therefore be scored in a criss-cross fashion with a sharp-tipped knife before you begin gluing.

Planing and filing

A file is required to remove small amounts of wood or plastic. As a general rule, it is used after sawing and before finishing the surface with glass (garnet) paper. Surform is a particularly good brand of tool (manufactured by Stanley Ltd) and offers a series of plane/files.

Blade replacement is easy and fairly cheap so do not be tempted to keep going to the bitter end with one tired old blade. When the blade is in good repair, the body of the Surform should quickly fill up with small shavings during use.

Right-handed people should hold the handle in their right hand and the spur in their left (Figure 28). When the blade is brand new, the spur should be held by the finger-tips as excessive downward pressure can cause the teeth to dig in and jam. However, as the blade nears the end of its useful life, or if you are tackling a particularly heavy job (e.g. a table surface, or using the tool as a paint-stripper) it may be necessary to apply downward pressure on the spur with the palm of the hand.

For light cuts or for smoothing a surface, the Surform should be used in the direction of the grain (direction A in Figure 28) but for large areas, the tool is at its most effective if the cut is made at about 30° to the direction of the grain, the tool still pointing in the direction of the grain, i.e. moving in a crab-like fashion (direction B in Figure 28).

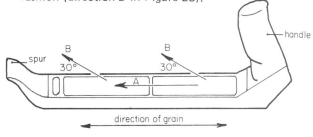

Figure 28 Movement of the Surform

Finishing

The importance of the final finishing operation cannot be over-emphasised. Patience and time expended at this stage will be well rewarded in terms of final quality. When a person first comes across someone else's work he looks, then touches. Both senses must be satisfied before real approval is forthcoming.

Iron-on edging strip

If you have used veneered or melamine-coated chipboard (particle board) you should finish the edges with the appropriate iron-on edging strip. Set your domestic iron thermostat at 'cotton'. Position the iron-on strip on the raw edge with a slight overhang at both edges if possible. Place the iron on the strip and move it along slowly (about 10 seconds for the iron to move its own length). Remove excess strip with medium-grade glass paper wrapped round a sanding-block.

Filling cracks and blemishes

There are many types of ready-made wood-filler on the market and if you can get a good colour match, use one of them. Ask your supplier for advice at the time of purchase and do not be afraid to show him a sample of the type of wood which you need to match. If you should have any difficulties, try a 'dust and glue' filler.

Place a sheet of glass paper, rough side up, on a flat surface and rub with a piece of scrap wood of the appropriate type. Collect the accumulated dust, and mix with just enough glue (PVA or waterproof type) to bind the dust together. Push the filler firmly into the crack with the flat edge of a screwdriver tip and leave to dry.

Smoothing the surface

Saw marks and large blemishes can be removed with the Surform. Otherwise use glass paper (medium grade) wrapped round a sanding-block.

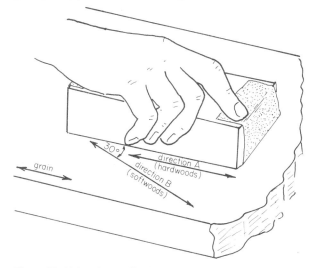

Figure 29 Using the sanding block

If you are sanding hardwood always rub with the grain (direction *A* in Figure 29). For softwood (e.g. red pine) the rubbing down should be done at about 30° to the grain (direction *B* in Figure 29). The latter method prevents the softest wood from being removed and leaving a heavy grain ripple.

Do not sand across the grain, especially if you intend using a varnish finish. You will leave small scratches which are indistinct at this stage, but infuriatingly obvious once the item is finished.

The surface should finally be rubbed down with fine glass or garnet paper.

An orbital sander will help with both these sanding operations, but do not regard it as essential, or as some sort of miracle machine. I no longer use one, preferring to choose the correct grade of abrasive paper and do the job by hand.

Varnishing

Varnish, or clear lacquer, normally comes in three types: gloss, semi-gloss (or silk), and matt. To the best of my knowledge, however, only gloss is sold in exterior grade. This apart, the choice is entirely a matter of personal taste.

Wipe down all surfaces with a damp cloth and leave for a few minutes to dry. Rub the brush with your finger-tips to remove any dust caught in the bristles. Apply a *thin* coat of varnish. (It is better to apply many thin coats than a few thick ones.)

When this coat is thoroughly dry, the surface will feel rough to the touch and both hardwoods and softwoods must once more be rubbed down in the direction of the grain with fine glass or garnet paper.

Two coats is the minimum that you can give to a fresh surface (good-quality violins and guitars receive from ten to twenty coats). The same procedure should be followed for each coat. The final coat, however, is best done as follows (see Figure 30):

(a) Apply a thin coat in the direction of the grain.

(b) Brush it across the grain to spread it. This applies only to large surfaces.

(c) 'Lay-off' by brushing in one direction only, with the brush at about 60° (Figure 31).

Painting

If you decide to use oil-based paints (i.e. non-emulsion) on any children's toys, be sure to use a non-toxic, lead-free variety.

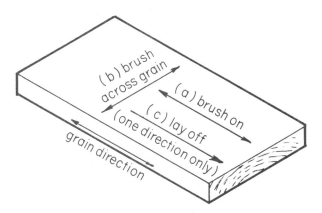

Figure 30 Applying the final coat of varnish

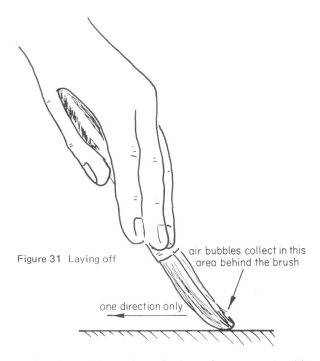

Figure 31 Laying off

air bubbles collect in this area behind the brush

one direction only

Starting with a clean fresh surface, you should apply the paint in the order given below, preparing and rubbing down between coats as for a varnish finish.

(a) Apply primer to seal the bare surface.

(b) Apply undercoat, which should be matched to the colour of the final coat.

(c) Apply the first coat of gloss.

(d) Apply the second coat of gloss. Lay-off with the brush as described for varnishing.

PROJECTS

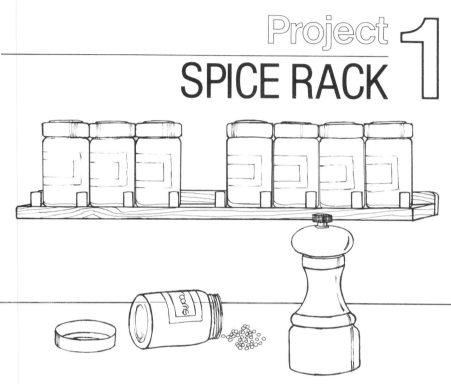

Project 1
SPICE RACK

Many kitchen condiments, including mustard, sauces, herbs and spices, are purchased in attractive glass containers, and it is handy to place these together on a small shelf specially made for the purpose. This small, lightweight shelf is a simple project on which to practise sawing and hammering techniques.

Materials

Item no.	Description	Quantity
1	dressed pine 45 x 12 x 400 mm (2 x $\frac{1}{2}$ nom x 16 in)	1
2	dressed pine 20 x 12 x 400 mm (1 x $\frac{1}{2}$ nom x 16 in)	1
3	hardwood dowel 6 mm diameter, 40 cm long ($\frac{1}{4}$ in diameter, 16 in long)	1

Item no.	Description	Quantity
4	oval brad nails 25 mm (1 in)	6
5	glass jars with plastic lids	6
6	PVA woodworder's adhesive	
7	varnish	

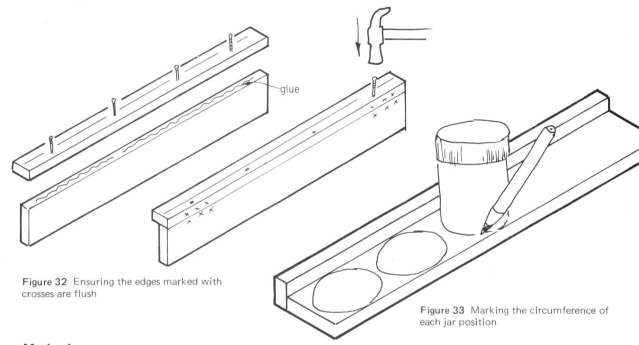

glue

Figure 32 Ensuring the edges marked with crosses are flush

Figure 33 Marking the circumference of each jar position

Method

1 Fix item 2 to item 1 with brad nails and glue. To determine the positions of the fixing nails, hold item 2 on top of item 1, keeping the edges flush with each other, and mark lightly in pencil the position of item 2. Hammer four nails into the centre of this strip, spacing them evenly and taking care to hold them as vertically as possible whilst hammering. You should just be able to feel the points of the nails coming through the wood. Spread glue along the edge of item 1; position item 2 against item 1 and make sure that the edges marked in the diagram with crosses are flush with each other. Hammer the nails home.

It is essential to take care during this operation. The nails are being hammered into a fairly thin section of wood, and it is likely that a nail which is not exactly vertical will burst through the surface. If this happens, stop hammering, and do not attempt to remove the nail until the glue has set. Check that the nails which have been inserted are holding the joint together — if the answer is 'yes', then they are doing what they are intended to do, and there is no need to use any more nails.

Wipe off any excess glue and leave for a few hours to dry.

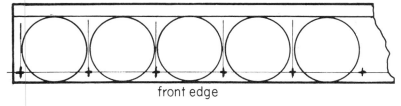

front edge

Figure 34 Marking the dowel positions

2 Use a jar to mark off the jar positions on the rack, then mark the retaining dowel positions. Ideally the position of the dowel is such that it touches each adjacent jar, while the jar itself is touching the back ledge, but if the positioning is gauged too tightly the jar may not fit at all if there is a slight error in measurement, so allow a small gap for safety. The dowel should be about 10 mm ($\frac{3}{8}$ in) from the front edge. Drill through each of these positions using a 6 mm ($\frac{1}{4}$ in) drill bit.

3 Drill a wall fixing hole, 4 mm ($\frac{3}{16}$ in) in diameter, at each end of the back ledge (marked A).

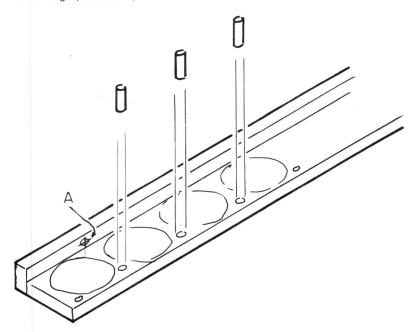

Figure 35 Drilling the wall fixing hole (A), and inserting the dowels

4 Cut the required number of 25 mm (1 in) dowel lengths. Remove the saw marks on the end of each dowel piece which will be seen, by sanding. Apply a little glue to the end of each dowel, then push each one firmly into each hole. Remove the excess glue.

5 Finish the rack as explained on page 20, using medium and fine garnet or glass paper, then varnish all over.

WINDMILL HERB RACK

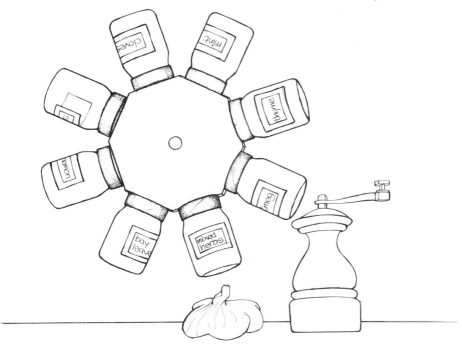

The windmill rack is based on an octagonal shape. The octagon and its centre position can easily be found by making a paper template and cutting a square block of wood to this shape. The lids of eight jars are fixed to each side, and the jars screwed onto them. When fixed to the wall, the rack rotates, so that the jar which is at the bottom can be unscrewed from its lid, and then screwed back again after use.

Figure 36 Making the paper template

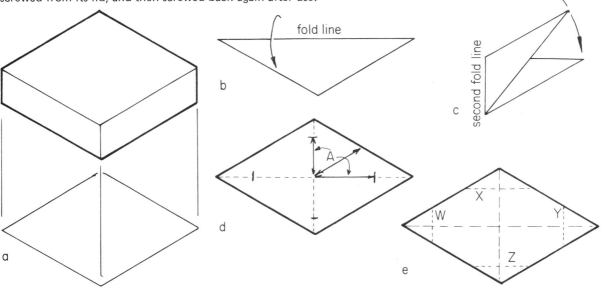

26

Materials

Item no.	Description	Quantity
1	dressed pine 120 x 45 x 120 mm (5 x 2 nom x $4\frac{7}{8}$ in)	1
2	dressed pine 45 x 20 x 75 mm (2 x 1 nom x 3 in)	1
3	screw and nut set with countersunk head 6 mm diameter, 75 mm long ($\frac{1}{4}$ in diameter, 3 in long)	1
4	round-headed screws (No. 8) 20 mm ($\frac{3}{4}$ in)	8
5	countersunk screws (for wall-mounting) (No. 8) 45 mm (2 in)	2
6	glass jars with screw-top lids	8
7	'Twin-pack' adhesive	
8	PVA woodworker's adhesive	
9	varnish	

Method

1 Make a paper template by cutting a sheet of paper to the same area as the larger of the two blocks or wood. Fold corner to corner across one diagonal, then fold across the second diagonal. Unfold the paper and measure the shortest distance from the centre to the edge (length A). Mark a point on each diagonal this distance away from the centre. Fold each diagonal at point A (lines W, X, Y and Z) then cut with scissors along these lines.

2 Position the template on the block and mark the template centre and the lines W, X, Y and Z on the block. Drill through the centre position (C) with a 6 mm ($\frac{1}{4}$ in) drill bit.

Figure 37 *Left* Marking the sawing lines for the octagonal block

Figure 38 Draw diagonals on each face to mark the lid positions

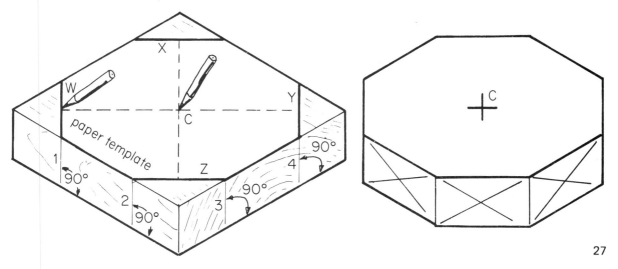

3 As a sawing guide, mark lines 1, 2, 3 and 4 as shown (continuing round the other side with lines 5, 6, 7 and 8). Use a square to ensure that the 90° angles are accurate. Saw along lines W, X, Y and Z (using lines 1 to 8 as sawing guides) then remove the saw marks with medium grade glass paper.

4 Lightly mark a cross on each of the eight faces, drawing from corner to corner; the centre point marks the position where each lid will be fixed.

5 Draw diagonals on the surface of the wall plate block and mark on these the centre, C, and two halfway positions, A and A. Drill the A positions through (for the wall-fixing screws) using a 4 mm ($\frac{3}{16}$ in) diameter drill, and the C position (for the pivot screw) with a 6 mm ($\frac{1}{4}$ in) diameter drill. Countersink the A screws on one side, and the C screw on the other side of the block, fixing the C screw with 'Twin-pack' glue according to the manufacturers' instructions.

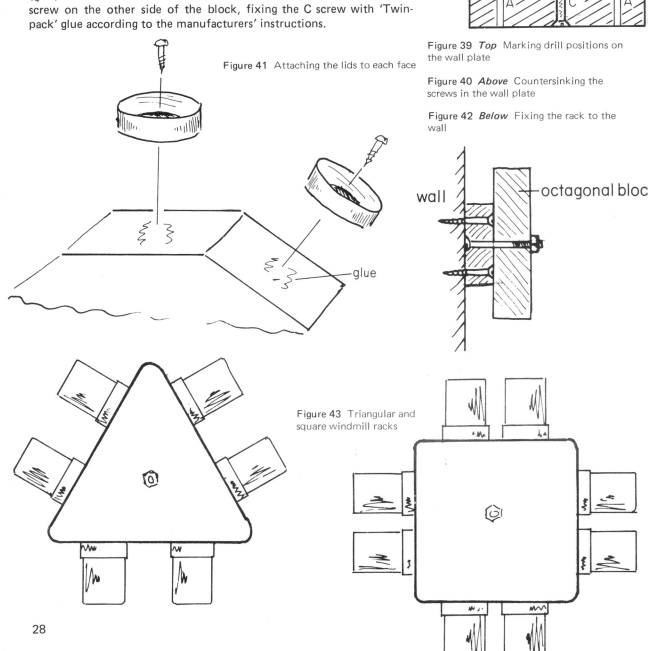

Figure 39 *Top* Marking drill positions on the wall plate

Figure 40 *Above* Countersinking the screws in the wall plate

Figure 42 *Below* Fixing the rack to the wall

Figure 41 Attaching the lids to each face

glue

wall

octagonal bloc

Figure 43 Triangular and square windmill racks

28

6 Drill through the lids of the jars with a 4 mm ($\frac{3}{16}$ in) drill — do not remove any sealing paper from the inside of the lid. Fix the lid to the octagonal block with 'Twin-pack' glue and 20 mm ($\frac{3}{4}$ in) round-headed screws (No. 8). Be careful not to overtighten the screws as this may break the lids.

7 Finish and varnish the rack.

8 Screw the wallplate to the wall, then screw the octagonal block to the plate (not too tightly).

Variations

An octagon is not of course the only shape that can be used for the rotating block. Experiment with triangular, square and other shapes, in varying sizes.

Project 3
CORNER SHELF

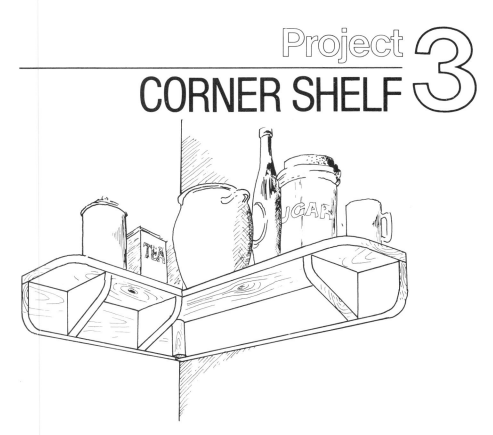

Flour, rice, pasta, dried beans — these type of foods add to the appearance and atmosphere of a kitchen if they are stored in large glass or earthernware containers. Such containers tend to be heavy, and a fairly substantial shelf is required to hold them and display them to best advantage.

A simple, straight shelf is easy to make, but often this will not make the best use of the kitchen's shape. A corner shelf is far more practical, and this is best made to the individual measurements of the corner, as house corners are rarely found to be exactly 90°; this is one reason why corner shelves are not usually available ready-made. The following instructions are for a shelf approximately 700 mm (30 in) long; the worker can easily adapt the information in order to make a straight shelf with brackets, if required.

Materials

Item no.	Description	Quantity
1	dressed pine 20 x 95 x 125 mm (1 x 4 nom x 5 in)	3
2	dressed pine 95 x 20 x 475 mm (4 x 1 nom x 17 in)	1
3	dressed pine 95 x 20 x 450 mm (4 x 1 nom x 18 in)	1
4	dressed pine 150 x 20 x 500 mm (6 x 1 nom x 20 in)	1
5	dressed pine 150 x 20 x 250 mm (6 x 1 nom x 10 in)	1
6	quarter-round hardwood beading (fillet) 25 x 25 x 90 mm (1 x 1 x $3\frac{1}{2}$ in)	2
7	oval brad nails 37 mm ($1\frac{1}{2}$ in)	30
8	round-headed screws (No. 8) 65 mm ($2\frac{1}{2}$ in) plus masonry fixing plugs	3
9	PVA woodworker's adhesive	
10	varnish	

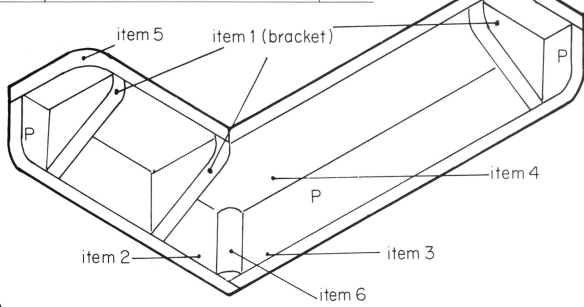

Figure 44 The position of each item of material in the final shelf: there are two pieces labelled item 6 — only one is visible in this diagram

item 5
item 1 (bracket)
P
P
item 4
P
item 2
item 3
item 6

Method

1 The brackets (item 1) should be bought ready cut, as an accurate 90° angle is required, and it is safer and easier to rely on the accuracy of the machinery used by the local wood supplier. To shape the brackets, mark a point 35 mm (1½ in) down from one corner, and join this point to the corner diagonally opposite. Hold the bracket firmly against a bench hook and saw along this cutting line. (When cutting a small piece of wood such as this, take extra care to keep the fingers away from the saw blade.) File the corner to give it a curved shape — the exact shape is unimportant on such a small curve.

2 Shape the end, front corners of the shelves to a well rounded curve, not only for aesthetic reasons, but also for reasons of safety. Shelves of this type are usually fixed at head height, and we are none of us very old before we realise that sharp corners versus skin and bone is an unfair match! Using a round container of appropriate dimensions as a template, mark the corner curve. Using a bench hook, remove as much material as possible with one straight saw cut, then file the wood down to the curved line.

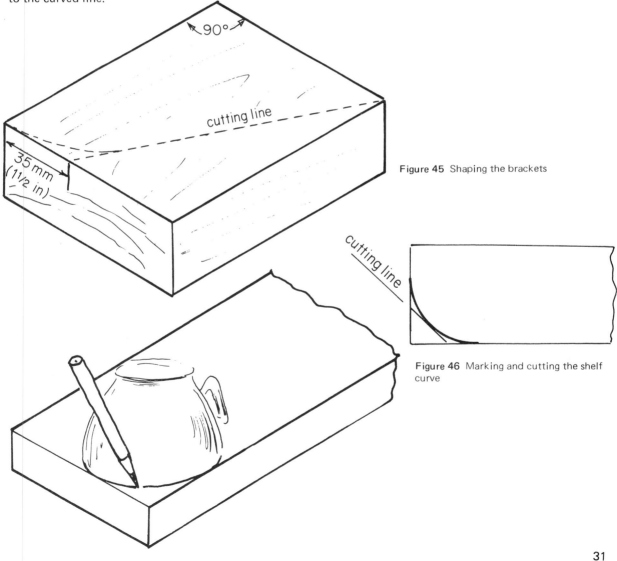

Figure 45 Shaping the brackets

Figure 46 Marking and cutting the shelf curve

31

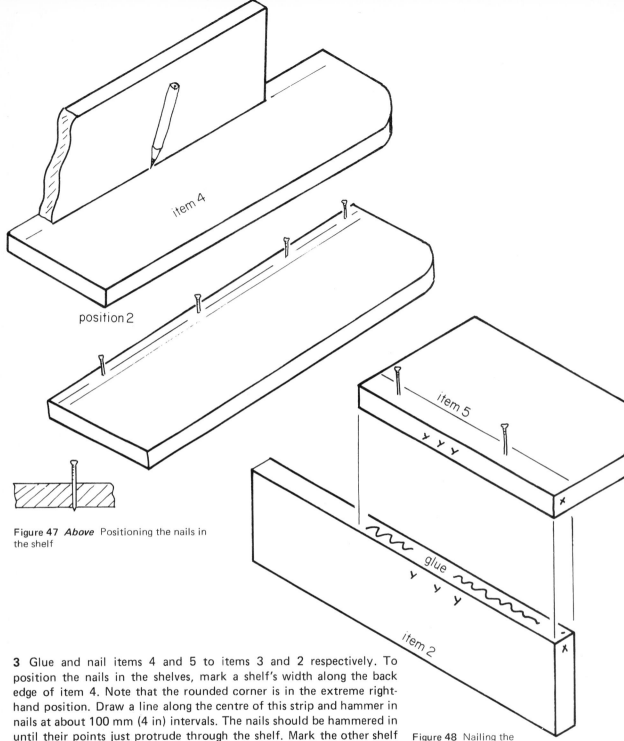

item 4

position 2

Figure 47 *Above* Positioning the nails in
the shelf

item 5

glue

item 2

Figure 48 Nailing the
shelf (item 5) into position

3 Glue and nail items 4 and 5 to items 3 and 2 respectively. To
position the nails in the shelves, mark a shelf's width along the back
edge of item 4. Note that the rounded corner is in the extreme right-
hand position. Draw a line along the centre of this strip and hammer in
nails at about 100 mm (4 in) intervals. The nails should be hammered in
until their points just protrude through the shelf. Mark the other shelf
(item 5) in the same way, but with the rounded corner in the lower left-
hand position (position 2).

4 To nail the shelf (item 5) in position, first apply glue to the upper
edge of item 2 and position the shelf carefully ensuring that the edges
marked X and YYY are flush. Ask a helper to hold the pieces firmly
during this operation. Hammer the nails home, and punch the heads
beneath the surface. Wipe off the excess glue.

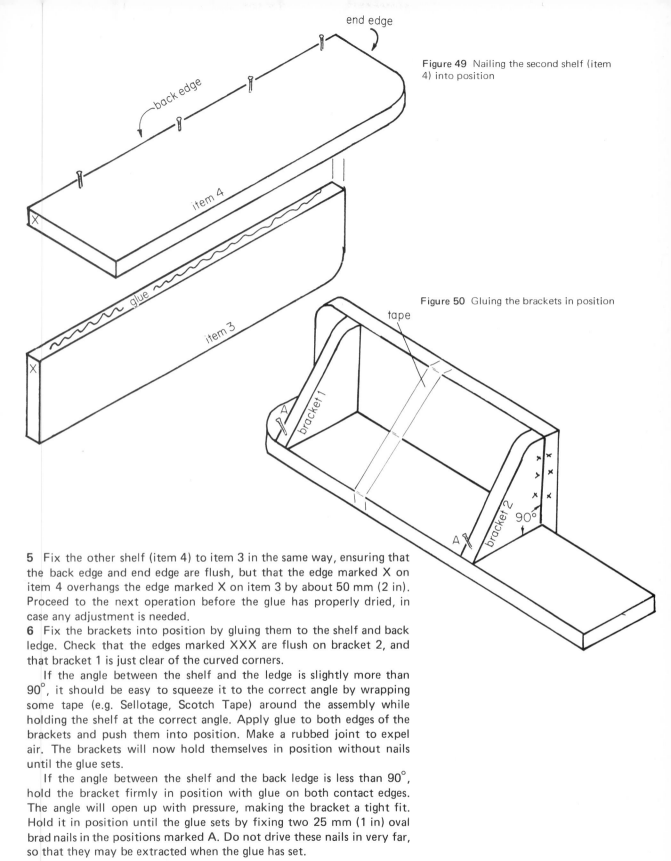

end edge

back edge

item 4

X

glue

item 3

X

Figure 49 Nailing the second shelf (item 4) into position

Figure 50 Gluing the brackets in position

tape

bracket 1

A

A

bracket 2

90°

5 Fix the other shelf (item 4) to item 3 in the same way, ensuring that the back edge and end edge are flush, but that the edge marked X on item 4 overhangs the edge marked X on item 3 by about 50 mm (2 in). Proceed to the next operation before the glue has properly dried, in case any adjustment is needed.

6 Fix the brackets into position by gluing them to the shelf and back ledge. Check that the edges marked XXX are flush on bracket 2, and that bracket 1 is just clear of the curved corners.

If the angle between the shelf and the ledge is slightly more than 90°, it should be easy to squeeze it to the correct angle by wrapping some tape (e.g. Sellotage, Scotch Tape) around the assembly while holding the shelf at the correct angle. Apply glue to both edges of the brackets and push them into position. Make a rubbed joint to expel air. The brackets will now hold themselves in position without nails until the glue sets.

If the angle between the shelf and the back ledge is less than 90°, hold the bracket firmly in position with glue on both contact edges. The angle will open up with pressure, making the bracket a tight fit. Hold it in position until the glue sets by fixing two 25 mm (1 in) oval brad nails in the positions marked A. Do not drive these nails in very far, so that they may be extracted when the glue has set.

7 Connect the shelves with the quarter-round beading (item 6). Smooth one end (A) of item 6, apply glue to both long flat sides, and fix it to the bracket by making a rubbed joint to expel air. Ensure that the edges marked X are flush, and that the beading is level with the lower edge of the shelf. Wipe off excess glue. Leave until the glue sets — at least 24 hours. The other shelf (item 4) will sit on top of this beading in the final assembly.

8 Since the unit is designed to fit into a particular corner of the room, check whether the corner is 90°, or whether it is more or less, using a piece of hardwood about 300 mm (12 in) square. Write 'corner' in one corner of the square, and push this into the corner of the room at the height at which the shelf is to be placed. If there is a gap, measure the gap and mark it on the board.

9 Working on a flat, firm surface, lay the two assembled parts together with a liberal layer of glue applied to the surfaces which will mate. Place the hardwood square on top (shown as a dotted line). If the angle is greater than 90°, hold the parts together as tightly as possible, and join them with a 37 mm (1½ in) oval brad nail at the position marked 1. Adjust the positions until the gap between the edge of the square and the back edge of the shelf corresponds to the wall gap. Hold the shelf firmly in this position, remove the square, and hammer 37 mm (1½ in) oval nails at the positions marked 2 and 3. Wipe off excess glue, and leave for several hours to allow the glue to set.

If the angle is less than 90°, hold the parts together firmly, check the gap, and hammer in the nails in the reverse order — 3, 2 and 1.

If there is a wedge-shaped gap at position A, fill this with woodfiller as part of the finishing operation.

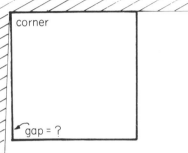

Figure 52 Gauging the corner angle of the room

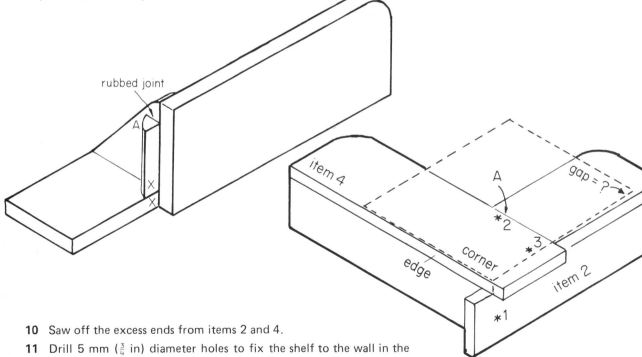

10 Saw off the excess ends from items 2 and 4.

11 Drill 5 mm (¾ in) diameter holes to fix the shelf to the wall in the positions marked P (Figure 44). Fix the shelf to the wall using round-headed screws (No. 8).

12 Finish and varnish the shelf.

Figure 53 Adjusting the shelf to fit the corner

SHELVING UNIT 4

A simple, sturdy bookshelf is within the capabilities of even the newest recruit to the ranks of the home carpenters, and is very economical to make. It is suitable for the lounge or study, and is particularly useful in a child's room where books and toys can be tidied away but still remain easily accessible.

Veneered or plastic-coated chipboard (particle board) can be used for reasons of economy, and the following size allows all the parts to be cut from two sheets of 12 mm ($\frac{1}{2}$ in) particle board, 1.8 m (6 ft) long and 225 mm (9 in) wide. It is important that all the shelves are the same length; mention this when the supplier is cutting the material to size and he will do his best to meet this requirement.

Materials

Item no.	Description	Quantity
1	veneered chipboard (particle board) 225 x 12 x 180 mm (9 x $\frac{1}{2}$ x 72 in)	2 sheets
2	hardboard 850 x 410 mm (34 x 16$\frac{1}{2}$ in)	1 sheet
3	quarter-round hardwood beading 25 x 25 x 170 mm (1 x 1 x 7 in)	6

Item no.	Description	Quantity
4	flat-headed woodscrews (No. 6) and cup washers 30 mm ($1\frac{1}{4}$ in)	12
5	panel pins 18 mm ($\frac{3}{4}$ in)	20
6	PVA woodworker's adhesive	
7	iron-on edging strip (optional) 600 mm (24 in)	
8	varnish (optional)	

Method

1 Cut the particle board into three shelf lengths and two side lengths.

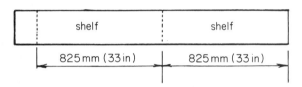

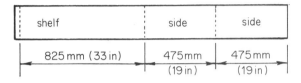

2 Lay the sides together on a flat surface. On each side mark 'top' and 'bottom' with pencil. Use a square to mark the lines A, B and C at 90° to the edge. These lines represent the position of the top surface of each shelf. (To achieve a large space below the middle shelf, move line B nearer to line C.)

3 To improve the strength of the corner joints, glue a piece of beading to each end of each shelf, placing it on the top side of the two lower shelves, and on the under side of the topmost shelf. Position the beading centrally, flush with the outside (short) edge, and mark its profile. Remove the beading and apply glue to the marked area. If the shelf is plastic-coated, key the surface (i.e. scratch closely in a criss-cross fashion to the full depth of the plastic) to improve its bonding quality. Position the beading, rubbing it a little to expel air bubbles. Leave it for 24 hours for the glue to set.

Figure 54 Cutting out the shelves and sides

Figure 55 *Left* Marking the shelf positions on the sides

Figure 56 *Below* Gluing beading to each end of the shelf

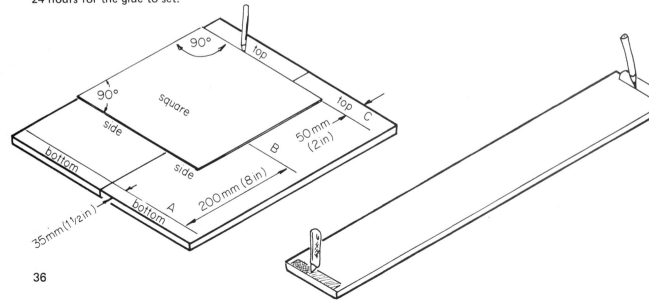

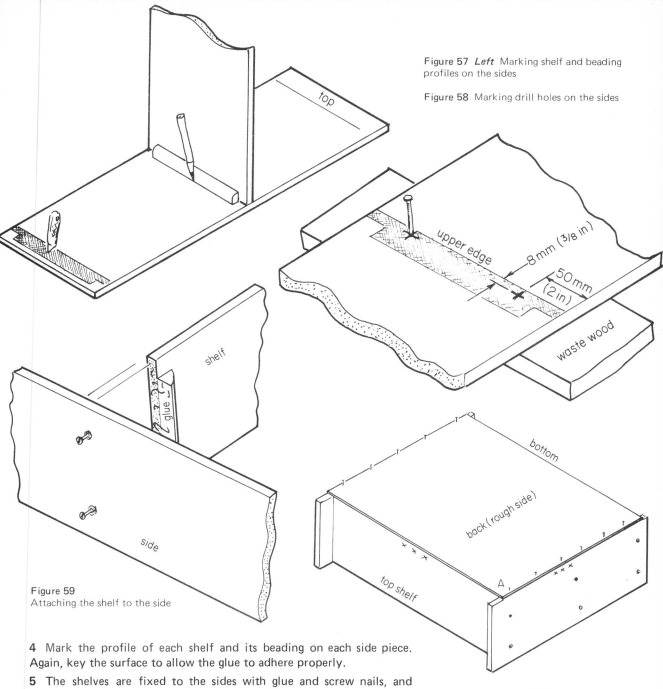

Figure 57 *Left* Marking shelf and beading profiles on the sides

Figure 58 Marking drill holes on the sides

top

upper edge

8 mm (3/8 in)

50 mm (2 in)

waste wood

shelf

glue

side

bottom

back (rough side)

top shelf

A

Figure 59
Attaching the shelf to the side

Figure 60 Fixing the back to the unit with panel pins

4 Mark the profile of each shelf and its beading on each side piece. Again, key the surface to allow the glue to adhere properly.

5 The shelves are fixed to the sides with glue and screw nails, and clearance holes for the screws should be drilled in the sides before final assembly. At each shelf position on each side piece, mark two points 50 mm (2 in) in from the edge and 8 mm ($\frac{3}{8}$ in) from the upper edge of the shelf. At each of these positions hammer an ordinary nail to a depth of 5 mm ($\frac{1}{4}$ in). You can now drill through the material with a 4 mm ($\frac{1}{8}$ in) drill bit without fear of the drill 'wandering'. Place waste wood beneath the material to avoid damaging the work surface.

6 Apply glue to the edge of the shelf and beading, and position it against the side piece. Ask a helper to hold the shelf in position while you drive the screws through the side and into the edge of the shelf. When glue oozes from the joint do not continue to tighten the screw, or the particle board will crumble, and an overtightened screw can exert no cramping force.

7 It is possible to leave the shelving unit without a backing, but this extra piece does greatly improve the allover rigidity of the design. Apply glue to the back edges of the shelves and sides (first keying them if necessary). Lay the backing (item 2) in position, ensuring that it is flush with the edges marked XXX on the side and top shelf. The shelves may have to be squeezed into shape to achieve a perfect fit. Adjust the top shelf and one side first, then check the fit on the other side. Hammer in the panel pins, then lay heavy weights along the back until the glue sets.

8 When the glue has set, round off the edges with a file. The backing can then be painted inside and outside with an emulsion paint if desired.

9 If using veneered chipboard, varnish the shelves, sides and (un-painted) backing. Finally apply the iron-on edging strip along the front edge of the shelves if required, following the manufacturers' instructions.

Project 5
FOOTSTOOL

After a hard day's work it's a welcome feeling to be able to put your feet up and slowly relax. The low, cushioned stool shown here is extremely comfortable when used as a footstool — large enough to support the calf muscles as well as the feet, and high enough to lift the legs to a horizontal position.

Materials

Item no.	Description	Quantity
1	dressed pine 95 x 20 x 400 mm (4 x 1 nom x 16 in)	2
2	dressed pine 95 x 20 x 440 mm (4 x 1 nom x 17¾ in)	2
3	dressed pine 70 x 20 x 275 mm (3 x 1 nom x 11 in) if this section is unavailable, use 95 x 20 x 275 mm (4 x 1 nom x 11 in)	4
4	hardboard 400 x 400 mm (max) (15⅞ x 15⅞ in)	1
5	dressed pine 20 x 20 x 150 mm (1 x 1 nom x 60 in)	1
6	upholstery foam 400 x 100 x 400 mm (15 x 4 x 15 in)	1
7	cushion cover fabric 135 (wide) x 50 cm (54 (wide) x 18 in)	1
8	oval brad nails 37 mm (1½ in)	40
9	panel pins 20 mm (¾ in)	20
10	countersunk wood screws (No. 8) 37 mm (1½ in)	12
11	PVA woodworker's adhesive	
12	glass (garnet) paper medium fine	1 sheet 1 sheet
13	varnish	

Method

1 First fit the legs to each end of the longer of the spars (item 2). Their positions should be marked one spar's width from the edge and one spar's width from the top. Use the width of either the legs of the other spars to help you mark these dimensions. Repeat for the other long spar (item 2).

2 The leg is fixed to item 2 with countersunk screws and glue. Fix the screw positions by marking a line at one end of each leg, at 90° to the edge, 75 mm (3 in) from the top. Use your square to do this. Mark the diagonals and on one of these diagonals mark three points, one 25 mm (1 in) from each end, and one in the centre. Drill through each of these positions with a 4.5 mm (3/16 in) diameter drill, and countersink each hole with a large drill bit.

3 Apply glue to the spar (item 2) over the area where it will be in con-

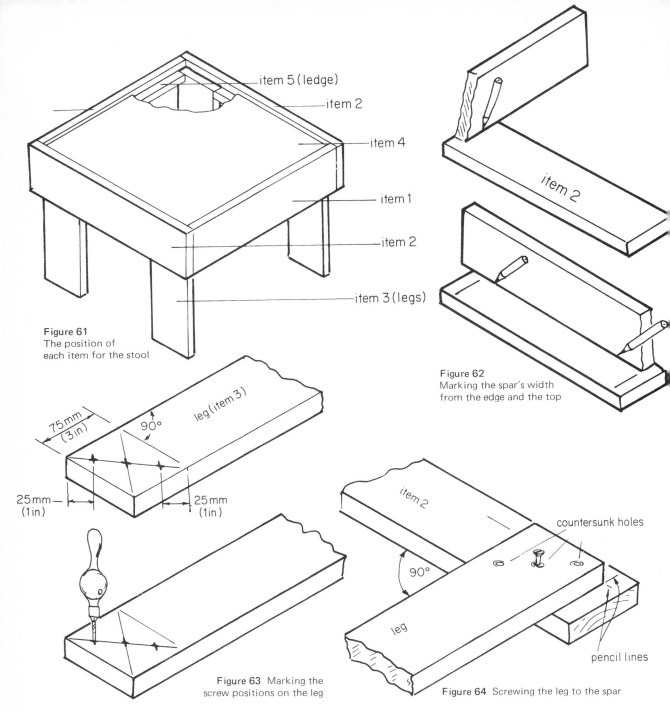

item 5 (ledge)

item 2

item 4

item 1

item 2

item 3 (legs)

Figure 61
The position of
each item for the stool

item 2

Figure 62
Marking the spar's width
from the edge and the top

leg (item 3)

75 mm
(3 in)

90°

25 mm
(1 in)

25 mm
(1 in)

Figure 63 Marking the
screw positions on the leg

item 2

countersunk holes

90°

leg

pencil lines

Figure 64 Screwing the leg to the spar

tact with the leg. Position the leg on the spar, carefully lining it up with the pencil lines. Then half hammer — half screw the 37 mm (1½ in) No. 8 screw fully home. The leg can still be moved fairly easily, so ensure, by using your square, that the right angle is in fact 90°. Then half hammer — half screw the remaining two screws fully home. Wipe off the excess glue. Repeat until all the legs are fixed in position.

4 The hardboard surface rests on ledges which are fitted to the spars. The top of each ledge is a spar's width from the top, i.e. 20 mm (1 in), and this position should be marked using a spar placed against the top edge of item 1 as shown.

40

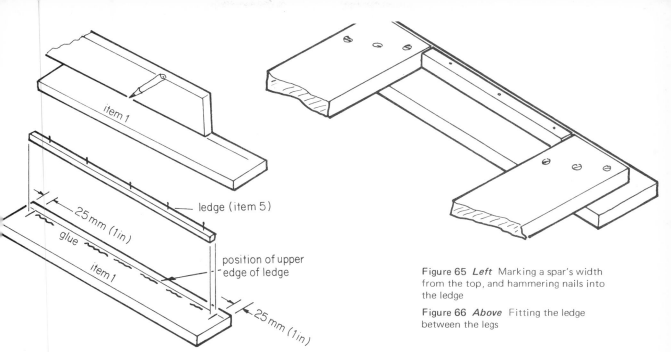

ledge (item 5)

25 mm (1 in)

glue

item 1

item 1

position of upper
edge of ledge

25 mm (1 in)

Figure 65 *Left* Marking a spar's width
from the top, and hammering nails into
the ledge

Figure 66 *Above* Fitting the ledge
between the legs

Cut the ledge to length, preferably on a sawboard, making it 50 mm (2 in) shorter than item 1. The ledge length should be 400 mm (16 in) but it is best to check it against the actual item to which it will be fitted.

Hammer four or five 37 mm ($1\frac{1}{2}$ in) oval brads into the ledge until you can just feel the points coming through the other side. Apply glue to item 1. Position the ledge 25 mm (1 in) from either end and hammer the nails home. Wipe off excess glue.

5 A ledge should also be fitted to item 2 as shown. Cut the ledge to fit between the legs — it does not have to be a neat fit. Mark a line on item 2, one spar's width from the top (as in Figure 66). Fix three or four 37 mm ($1\frac{1}{2}$ in) oval brad nails half way into the ledge. Apply glue to item 2 (the spar). Position the ledge. Hammer the nails home and wipe off excess glue.

6 The top (item 4) is meant, of course, to support the cushion, but it also has a very important function during assembly — to keep the stool angles at 90° when viewed from the top (Figure 67).

Therefore, the top must be ready to fit immediately the corners of the stool have been fixed, before the glue sets. Corners which are not quite 90° can then be adjusted without fear of straining or breaking a completed corner joint.

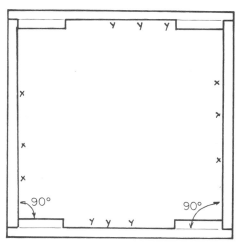

unglued corner

Figure 67 The top keeps the stool corners at 90°

Figure 68 *Left and below* Marking the position of the corner nail on item 2

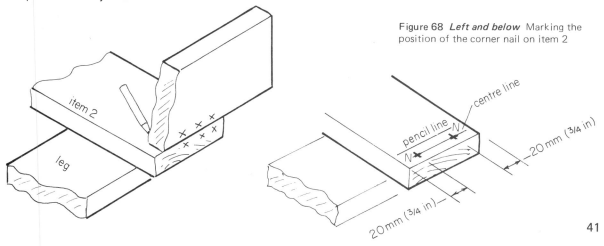

item 2

leg

centre line

pencil line

20 mm (3/4 in)

20 mm (3/4 in)

41

Hold the stool together by hand, and make sure that the top sits on the ledge. It may be a little loose, that is acceptable.

7 Now the position of the corner nail in the spar (item 2) must be fixed.

Hold a spar in position on item 2, (see Figure 68) and after ensuring that the edges marked *xxx* are flush, draw a pencil line as shown.

Draw a line down the centre of this strip (see Figure 68) — great accuracy is not required. 20 mm ($\frac{3}{4}$ in) from each end of this line, mark the nailing positions (marked *N* on the figure).

8 The nail positions on the spars (item 1) differ slightly from those just described for item 2.

On item 1 lightly mark 'top' on one edge.

Mark a spar's width strip up the side (Figure 69) and a centre line on this strip as previously described.

This time, the nail positions *N* (in Figure 97b) are marked 35 mm ($1\frac{1}{2}$ in) from the top edge and 20 mm ($\frac{3}{4}$ in) from the bottom.

Repeat this for both ends of the two spars (item 1).

9 Hardboard, although a very thin material, is fairly difficult to nail into (as its name might imply). It is therefore best to fix the 20 mm ($\frac{3}{4}$ in) panel pins in position beforehand, with the points just piercing the board.

Using one of the slats (item 1) mark the ledge position all round the top of the smooth side of the hardboard. Use about three or four nails per edge.

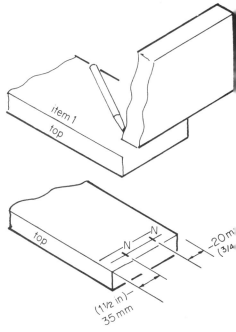

Figure 69 Marking the position of the nails on item 1

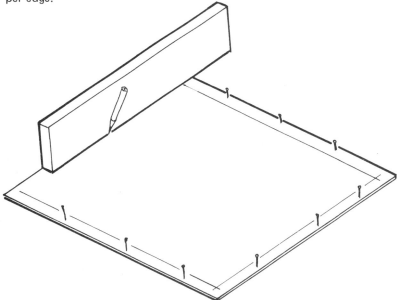

Figure 70 Marking the positions of the panel pins on the smooth side of the hardboard

10 For this operation you will probably require a helper to hold the joint in position while you nail it.

Apply glue to the mating edges and hold the joint firmly in position.

Use 37 mm ($1\frac{1}{2}$ in) oval brad nails, nailed vertically into the positions labelled *N* in Figure 71. Punch the nails below the surface (see Nailing, page 14).

Carefully support the joint and turn the job round.

Nail two oval brads vertically into the two nail positions shown on that face (Figure 71 bottom).

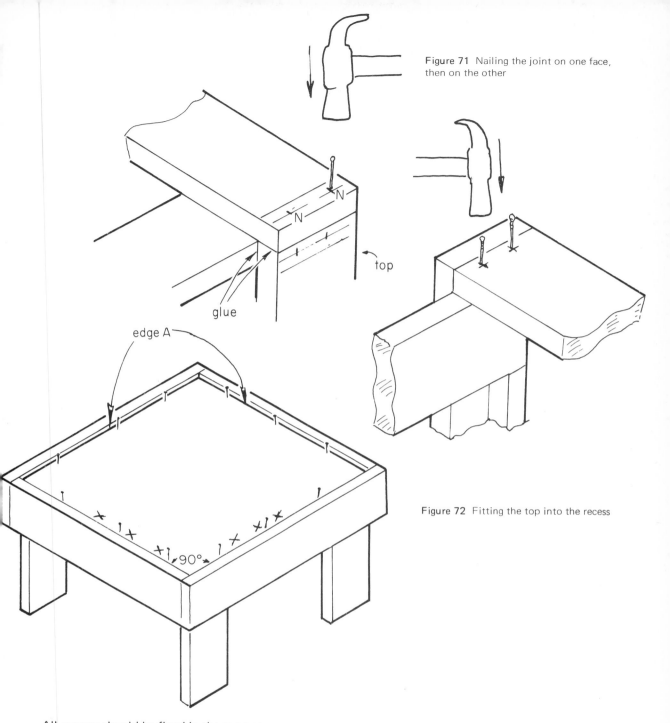

Figure 71 Nailing the joint on one face, then on the other

top

glue

edge A

90°

Figure 72 Fitting the top into the recess

All corners should be fixed in the same manner.

Take care to support the joints when the assembly is being moved about, since they can be easily strained if they are moved excessively *before the glue sets*.

11 Apply glue to the ledge and place the top in position (Figure 100).

If the top is a fairly loose fit, make sure that there is no gap along two adjacent edges (marked *xxx* in Figure 72) thus ensuring 90° angles at the corners.

Hammer the nails home.

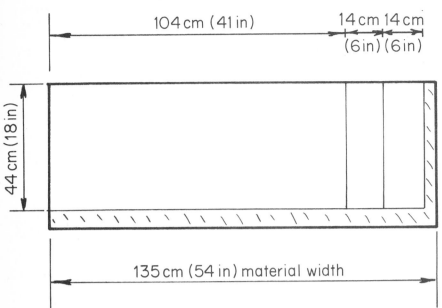

104 cm (41 in)   14 cm (6 in) 14 cm (6 in)

44 cm (18 in)

135 cm (54 in) material width

Figure 73 Cutting the fabric for the cushion

12 The layout for cutting the upholstery fabric is shown in Figure 73.

13 Foam should be covered in the following manner.

Wrap the material round the piece of foam , right side of material towards the foam. Pull the material tightly and tack the seam (see Figure 74). (The material must be tightly stretched or it will wrinkle badly during use.) Remove the material from the foam and machine or hand-sew the seam.

14 Gently pull the material (wrong side nearest the foam) on to the cushion. Place the seam along the lower back edge. Now turn under 2 cm ($\frac{3}{4}$ in) right round the edge of the end of the cushion (Figure 75).

15 Place the end piece of material on the end of the cushion, and tuck the seam allowance under the main cushion material (Figure 76). Pin and tack. Hand-sew with small stitches. Repeat for the other end, this time pulling the material very tight. Pin all round, tack and hand-sew.

Cover the other pieces of foam in the same way.

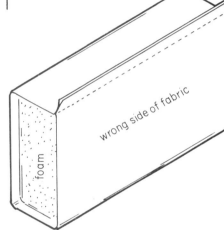

Figure 74 Tack the seam along one edge

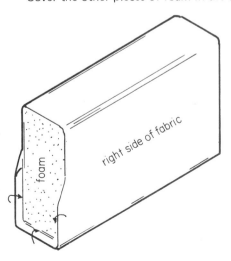

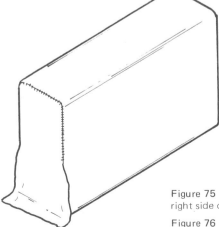

Figure 75 *Far left* Draw the cover on, right side outermost

Figure 76 *Left* Hand-sew the end flaps

MULTI-PURPOSE TABLE 6

This style of table is suitable as a stand for a television or record player and records. It can be used for coffee or drinks, or even as an occasional stool if a cushion is laid on top.

It is perhaps one step removed from what I would regard as true 'coarse' carpentry (items held together by glue, nails, and screws), but nevertheless its construction is fairly straightforward in spite of the dowel joints.

Materials

Item no.	Description	Quantity
1	dressed pine 35 x 35 x 400 mm ($1\frac{1}{2}$ x $1\frac{1}{2}$ nom x 16 in)	4
2	dressed pine 35 x 35 x 280 mm ($1\frac{1}{2}$ x $1\frac{1}{2}$ nom x $11\frac{1}{4}$ in)	4
3	dressed pine 35 x 20 x 480 mm ($1\frac{1}{2}$ x 1 x 18 in)	4
4*	9.5 mm ($\frac{3}{8}$ in) hardwood dowel x 600 mm (24 in)	1
5	wood-veneered, plastic-coated or untreated 12 mm ($\frac{1}{2}$ in) chipboard (particle board) 300 x 450 mm (12 x 18 in)	2

Item no.	Description	Quantity
6	65 mm (2½ in) No. 8 countersunk woodscrews and cup washers	8
	or 65 mm (2½ in) No. 8 dome head brass wood screws (no cup washers)	
	PVA woodworker's adhesive	
	varnish	
	garnet or glass paper medium	1 sheet

*If your drill chuck will not accept a drill bit of 9.5 mm ($\frac{3}{8}$ in), then you should use the biggest drill bit that will be accepted and purchase hardwood dowel in that size.

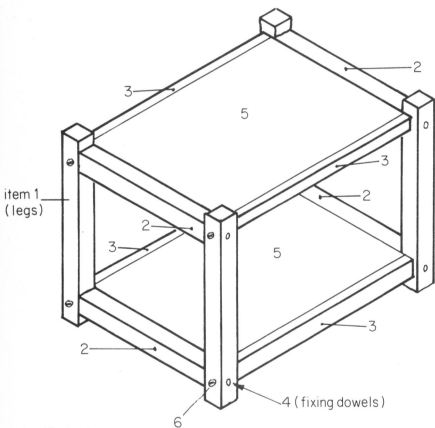

item 1
(legs)

Figure 77 Construction plan of the table

4 (fixing dowels)

Method

1 Unless you happen to have, or can borrow a pair of sash cramps, then for this project you will have to make the simple and very useful cramping device shown in Figure 80. (For construction details see Tools, page 13.)

The spars (items 3) are simply glued and cramped (no screws or nails required) to the boards (items 5).

The top and bottom are exactly the same so the following instructions are 'times two'.

46

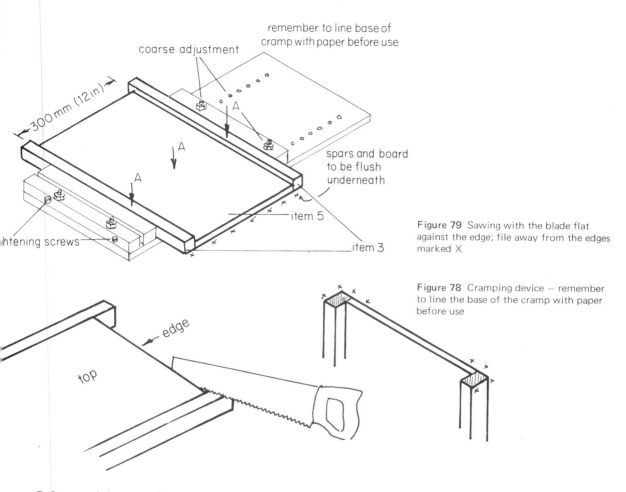

remember to line base of
cramp with paper before use

coarse adjustment

300 mm (12 in)

A

A

A

spars and board
to be flush
underneath

item 5

...htening screws

item 3

Figure 79 Sawing with the blade flat
against the edge; file away from the edges
marked X

Figure 78 Cramping device — remember
to line the base of the cramp with paper
before use

edge

top

Before applying any glue, set the coarse adjustment bar (see Tools, page 13) and line the base of the cramp with paper.

Apply glue along the edges of the board where they meet the spars and place all in the cramp as in Figure 78.

First check that you are gluing against the concave side of the spar if it is at all bowed.

Since items 3 are a little longer than the board (this is by design at this stage) the ends of the spars can only be flush at one end during the cramping operation. If you find that during the cramping the glued joint slips, arrange for one end to be flush, and hold the joint together by hand in the cramp and leave for twenty minutes before cramping to allow partial setting of the PVA glue to take place.

Push firmly down in the direction of the arrows A (see Figure 78) during final cramping, as this ensures that the spars and the board are flush underneath, i.e. on the top surface of the finished table.

Leave in cramp for 4-6 hours for the glue to set.

2 When the glue has completely set, remove the boards from the cramps and trim off the excess spar at one end (the other end was cramped flush). First saw off as much as possible, resting the board on your saw-board (see Tools, page 11) and working from the top. This ensures that any ragged edge which results from the sawing operation is on the unseen underside. The flat edge of the saw should be against the flat edge of the board while you are sawing to ensure a true cut.

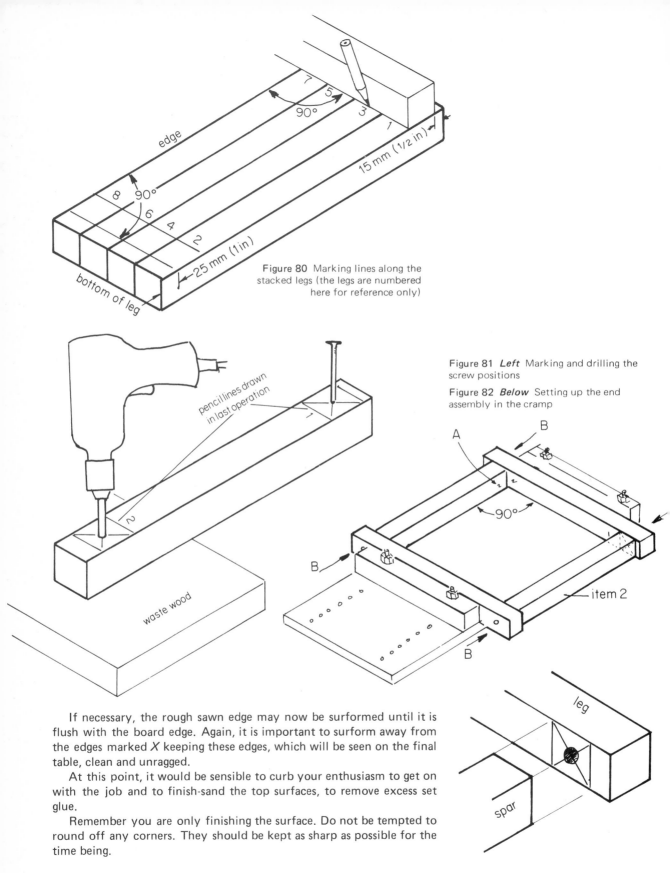

Figure 80 Marking lines along the stacked legs (the legs are numbered here for reference only)

Figure 81 *Left* Marking and drilling the screw positions

Figure 82 *Below* Setting up the end assembly in the cramp

If necessary, the rough sawn edge may now be surformed until it is flush with the board edge. Again, it is important to surform away from the edges marked *X* keeping these edges, which will be seen on the final table, clean and unragged.

At this point, it would be sensible to curb your enthusiasm to get on with the job and to finish-sand the top surfaces, to remove excess set glue.

Remember you are only finishing the surface. Do not be tempted to round off any corners. They should be kept as sharp as possible for the time being.

48

3 Now mark the position of the spars (item 2) on the legs (item 1).

Stack the legs together on a flat surface as shown in Figure 80.

Mark out all the legs together.

First, mark lines 25 mm (1 in) from the bottom and 15 mm ($\frac{1}{2}$ in) from the top at 90° to the edge. Use your square for this operation.

Then, without moving the legs, lay one of the spars (item 2) against the lines, and draw a second line to give two stripes, each the width of the spars.

For future reference, mark lightly, in the positions shown in Figure 82, the reference numbers 1-8.

4 Mark the diagonals on the squares, at the top and bottom of each leg which mark the spar positions. At each crossing point of the diagonals (Figure 81) hammer in a nail for about 6 mm ($\frac{1}{4}$ in) and then remove it by hand. This gives the drill a start and eliminates the possibility of drill wander.

Then drill through on to waste wood in each of these positions 9.5 mm ($\frac{3}{8}$ in) diameter, keeping the drill as vertical as possible.

Repeat for all four legs.

5 Set up the legs (item 1) and the spars (item 2) in the cramp to form the shape of an end assembly (Figure 82). The end of the spars should butt against the diagonal markings as shown in Figure 84b.

Mark the same reference numbers on the spars as are on the legs (i.e. nos. 1-8).

In Figure 82 you can see a number 2 (indicated by arrow) has been marked to correspond with the 2 on the leg. This numbering is very important to ensure correct assembly.

Use your square to check that the angles are all 90°.

Using a 9.5 mm ($\frac{3}{8}$ in) diameter drill, drill through the existing holes in the legs into the spars in the direction of the arrows labelled *B* in Figure 82. If your drill chuck will not accept a 9.5 mm ($\frac{3}{8}$ in) diameter drill bit then you should use the biggest drill bit that will be accepted. The hardwood dowel (item 4) must be the same diameter as the drill used. The drill should enter to a total depth of 65 mm ($2\frac{1}{2}$ in). A piece of tape on the drill bit, 65 mm ($2\frac{1}{2}$ in) from the tip will act as a depth gauge.

Repeat this drilling operation in all four corners and for both end assemblies.

6 Cut the 9.5 mm ($\frac{3}{8}$ in) diameter hardwood dowel into 75 mm (3 in) lengths and taper one end slightly so that it will easily enter the drilled holes. This is very easily done using an ordinary pencil sharpener (Figure 83).

Making sure that the reference numbers match up on the legs and spars, apply glue to the dowel and hammer it into the leg.

Apply glue to the end surface of the spar and insert some into the 9.5 mm ($\frac{3}{8}$ in) diameter hole in the spar.

Now hammer the dowel through the leg into the end of the spar.

When it is fully home, the dowel should still stick out a little. This extra piece will be trimmed off later.

Do the reference numbers still match?

Cramp the end assembly as shown in Figure 84b and check all 90° angles. If they are slightly off, slacken the cramp a little and adjust the assembly to correct the angles.

Wipe off excess glue and leave overnight to set.

Repeat for the other end assembly.

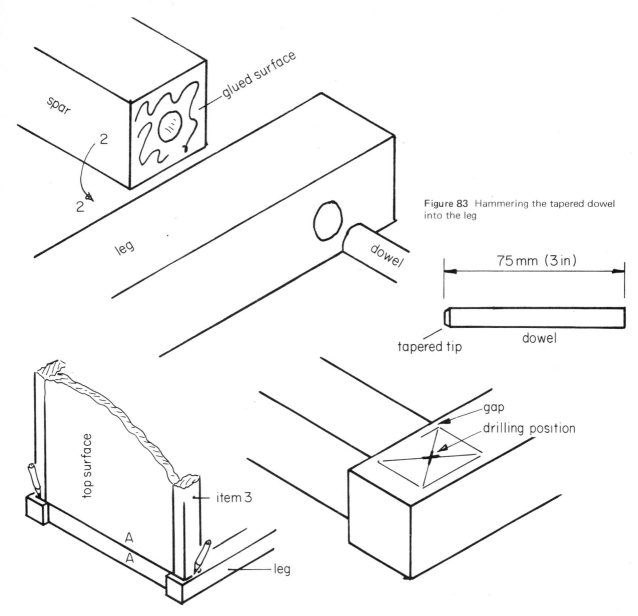

spar

glued surface

2

2

leg

dowel

Figure 83 Hammering the tapered dowel into the leg

75 mm (3 in)

tapered tip

dowel

top surface

item 3

A
A

leg

gap

drilling position

7 You must now decide which surface is the top and which the bottom, which part goes to the front and which to the rear of the finished table. The principle here is that the least perfect edge goes to the bottom rear and of course the most perfect to the top front.

Having decided, mark corresponding letters or numbers on the surfaces and end assemblies — in Figure 84 the letter *A* has been used.

The end assemblies are to be fixed to the surfaces using screws into the surface spars (items 3) and the positions of these surface spars on the end assembly must be ascertained.

The surfaces are rested against the end assemblies (Figure 84) and the spar positions are marked with a pencil.

Note that there is a gap between the surface spar and the edge of the leg (Figure 84). You should make sure that this gap is the same at both ends.

Figure 84 *Left and above* Marking the position of the surface against the end assembly

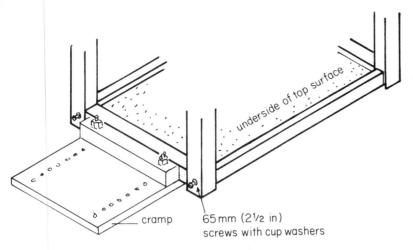

Figure 85 Pressing the top surface and end assemblies in the cramp

cramp

65 mm (2½ in) screws with cup washers

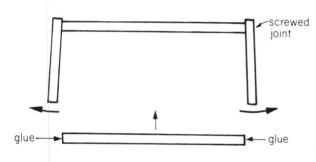

Figure 86 Fixing the bottom surface

screwed joint

glue

glue

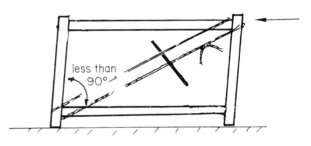

less than 90°

Figure 87 Using a Spanish windlass to correct the 90° angle

Mark diagonals on the position occupied by the end spar and where they cross drill through, onto waste wood, with a 5 mm ($\frac{3}{16}$ in) diameter drill (Figure 84).

There are eight such holes to be drilled.

8 Set up the cramp to accept the end assemblies and surfaces as in Figure 85, and line the base of the cramp with paper.

Apply glue to the edges of the top surface and set up as in Figure 86 by pressing both end end assemblies, and the surface, firmly down on to the cramp. During the cramping you must ensure that the top surface and the spars will be flush. Tighten the cramp and screw in the four screws (two per end) with cup washers.

Remove the cramp and wash it to remove excess glue.

9 When fitting the bottom surface, which is done in exactly the same way as the top surface fitting, it will be necessary to spread the ends slightly to get the surface in position. Do not overdo this or you will strain and possibly damage the previously screwed joints.

If the finished job is slightly lopsided (Figure 87), simply push it over until a 90° angle is achieved and hold it in that position by a length of rope. Figure 88b illustrates a Spanish windlass which can be tightened by turning the stick, thus twisting the rope.

Leave it for 24 hours until the glue has completely set.

Finish and varnish (see Finishing and Varnishing, page 20).

TWO-SEATER SETTEE 7

This is a lightweight design, which is very economical due to the relatively thin section of material used.

It is not recommended that the length be extended to make a three- or four-seater settee unless you use thicker material, but it would, of course, be possible to reduce the size to make a single armchair.

For reasons of economy, as well as appearance, no cushions have been included in the arm positions. You may, however, add these by reducing the length of the seat cushion accordingly.

Materials

Item no.	Description	Quantity
1	dressed pine 95 x 20 x 575 mm (4 x 1 nom x 23 in)	4
2	dressed pine 95 x 20 x 550 mm (4 x 1 nom x 22 in)	4
3	dressed pine 95 x 20 mm x 1.2 m (4 x 1 in nom x 4 ft)	2
4	dressed pine 45 x 20 mm x 1.1 m (2 x 1 in nom x 3 ft 8 in)	2

Item no.	Description	Quantity
5	dressed pine 45 x 45 x 95 mm (2 x 2 nom x $3\frac{3}{4}$ in)	4
6	dressed pine 95 x 20 x 665 mm (4 x 1 nom x $26\frac{3}{4}$ in)	9
7	dressed pine 275 x 20 mm x 1.195 m (9 x 1 in nom x 3 ft $11\frac{3}{4}$ in)	1
8*	aluminium alloy angle bar 35 x 35 x 3 mm thick ($1\frac{1}{2}$ x $1\frac{1}{2}$ x $\frac{1}{8}$ in thick)	2
	No 8 x 50 mm (2 in) countersunk screws and cup washers	16
	No. 10 x 25 mm (1 in) countersunk screws and cup washers	4
	37 mm ($1\frac{1}{2}$ in) oval brad nails	100 approx
	6 mm ($\frac{1}{4}$ in) diameter x 30 mm ($1\frac{1}{4}$ in) long round head screws, nails and washers	4 sets
	PVA woodworker's adhesive	
	garnet or glass paper medium fine	2 sheets 2 sheets
	varnish	
	2 m (6 ft) long 9.5 mm ($\frac{3}{8}$ in) diameter dowel rod. (If you do not have a 9.5 mm ($\frac{3}{8}$ in) diameter chuck on your drill, you must buy the dowel diameter equal to the biggest drill bit that your chuck will accept.)	1
	100 mm (4 in) Upholstery foam *base* 500 mm x 1.2 m (1 ft 8 in x 4 ft) *back* 400 mm x 1.2 m (1 ft 4 in x 4 ft)	
	fabric to cover cushions 135 cm wide, 2.5 m long (54 in wide, $2\frac{1}{2}$ yd long)	

*Mild steel can be used if aluminium alloy is unobtainable.

If you have not already done so, you should make the adjustable cramp described on page 53. The alternative is to buy or borrow a fairly expensive commercial sash cramp. If you decide on this latter course of action, you will need two cramps with a maximum cramping dimension of 750 mm (2 ft 6 in).

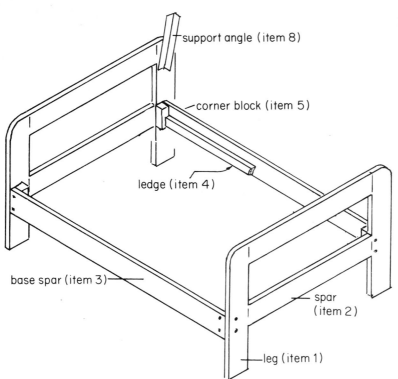

Figure 88 Construction of the settee —
the slats for the base (item 6) and the back
rest (item 7) are not shown

Method

1 The final positions of the spars (item 2) should be marked on the
edge of each leg (item 1). Mark one end of each leg with a letter 'T' to
signify 'top'. Stack the legs together as shown in Figure 53a keeping the
ends (marked *X* in the figure) flush. The letters *T* should then all be at
the same end.

Lay a spar across the legs (Figure 89) with its edge flush with the
ends of the legs. Mark the spar position as indicated.

Now mark a line 275 mm (11 in) from the top at 90° to the edge
(Figure 53b). Use your square for this operation (see Tools, page 11).

Now lay the spar against this line and mark the position of the other
edge of the spar on every leg.

2 Lay the end assemblies out together on the floor and mark numbers
1-8 in pairs on each joining corner (see Figure 90).

If you find at any stage during assembly that these numbers do not
match — stop, . . . think, and get things sorted out before proceeding.

Figure 89 Marking the final positions of
the spars

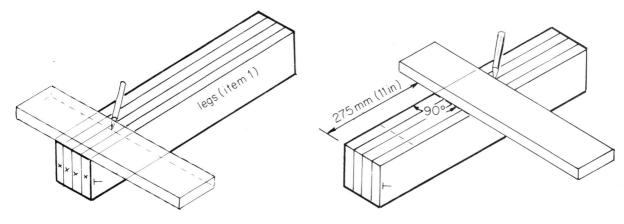

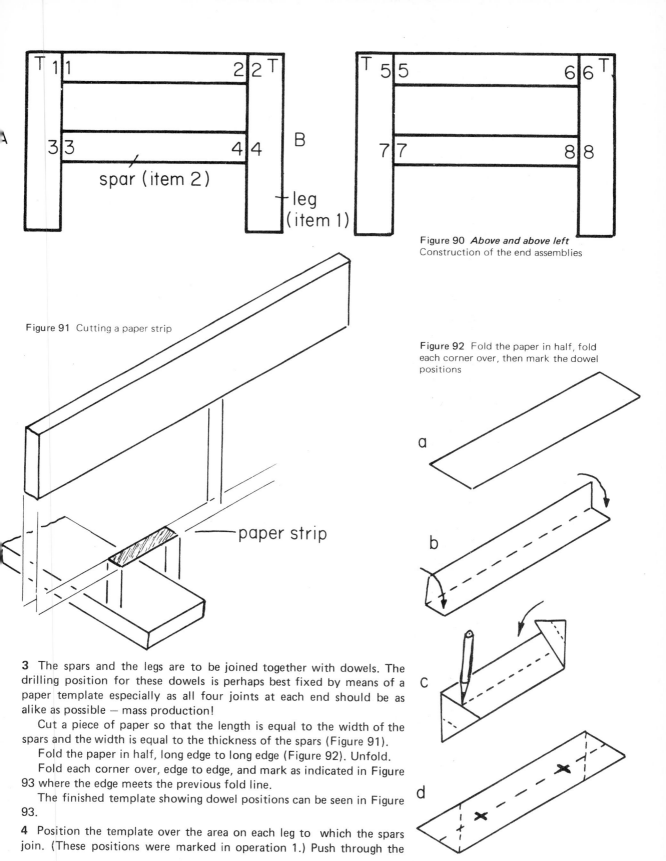

A

B

spar (item 2)

leg (item 1)

Figure 90 *Above and above left*
Construction of the end assemblies

Figure 91 Cutting a paper strip

paper strip

Figure 92 Fold the paper in half, fold
each corner over, then mark the dowel
positions

a

b

c

d

3 The spars and the legs are to be joined together with dowels. The drilling position for these dowels is perhaps best fixed by means of a paper template especially as all four joints at each end should be as alike as possible — mass production!

Cut a piece of paper so that the length is equal to the width of the spars and the width is equal to the thickness of the spars (Figure 91).

Fold the paper in half, long edge to long edge (Figure 92). Unfold.

Fold each corner over, edge to edge, and mark as indicated in Figure 93 where the edge meets the previous fold line.

The finished template showing dowel positions can be seen in Figure 93.

4 Position the template over the area on each leg to which the spars join. (These positions were marked in operation 1.) Push through the

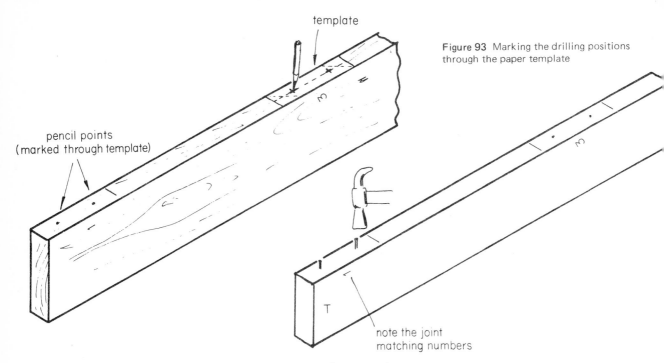

template

Figure 93 Marking the drilling positions through the paper template

pencil points
(marked through template)

note the joint
matching numbers

template at each drilling point with a sharp pencil (Figure 56). There are four drilling positions on each leg. In each of these positions, hammer a 25 mm (1 in) oval brad nail, half way in. Keep the nails as vertical as you possibly can.

5 This part of the work must be done on a firm, flat surface.

Each spar should be held down firmly — kneeling on it is quite effective — and the leg should be presented to the spar. Ensure that the joint matching numbers match and that the spar lines up with its final position as described in operation 2 above.

Use a square to make sure that these items are at 90° to each other.

The leg must also be held down on the flat surface and the joint should be closed with gentle hammer taps against a piece of scrap wood to protect the leg. Take the joint apart and remove the nails using the claw part of your hammer. Both nail heads should have left a clear imprint on the end of the spar.

Repeat this for every joint — eight in all.

6 Wrap a piece of tape round a 9.5 mm ($\frac{3}{8}$ in) drill, at a height of 30 mm ($1\frac{1}{4}$ in) to act as a depth gauge. (If your drill chuck does not take a drill of this size, then use the biggest drill that it will take. The dowels used in the joints must match the size of drill being used.) Drill to a depth of 30 mm ($1\frac{1}{4}$ in) on each of the nail and nail head marks. This should be done as vertically as possible. The piece of wood being drilled should be held by a helper against some solid object to keep it vertical. Your 'apprentice' can also keep an eye on the drill and tell you if you are going off the true line.

There should be four holes on each leg, and four on each spar (two per end).

7 Set the coarse adjustment on your cramp (see Tools, page 12) to fit across the faces marked 'cramp' in Figure 96.

Cut sixteen dowels, each 55 m ($2\frac{1}{4}$ in) long and taper the ends slightly, as shown in Figure 60. This can be done by rubbing with glass paper or by using a pencil sharpener.

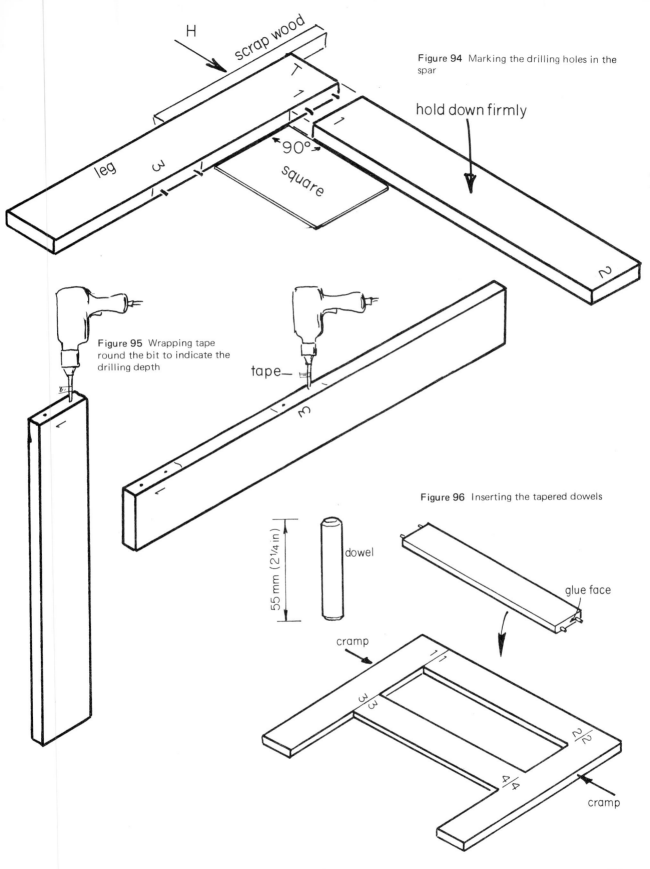

H
scrap wood
T
hold down firmly
leg
3
square
90°

Figure 94 Marking the drilling holes in the spar

Figure 95 Wrapping tape round the bit to indicate the drilling depth

tape

Figure 96 Inserting the tapered dowels

55 mm (2¼ in)
dowel

glue face

cramp

cramp

57

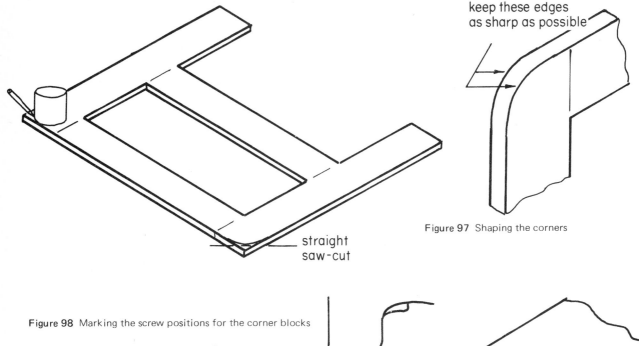

keep these edges
as sharp as possible

Figure 97 Shaping the corners

straight
saw-cut

Figure 98 Marking the screw positions for the corner blocks

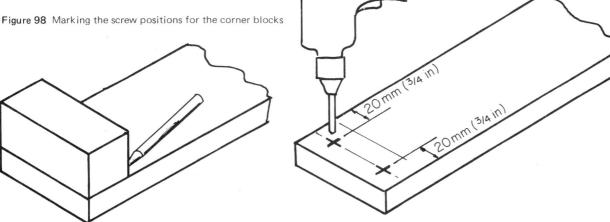

20 mm (3/4 in)

20 mm (3/4 in)

Work on one end assembly at a time. Make sure that the number marking is correct before you start. Squeeze some glue into each hole on the spars and push a dowel into each one.

Now drop some glue into each dowel hole on the legs, and apply a liberal layer of glue to the ends (marked 'glue face' in Figure 96). There are four glue faces in all.

Assemble the end pushing the joints part way home by hand.

Position in the cramp across the faces marked 'cramp' in Figure 96, and tighten the cramp until glue is oozing from all of the joints.

Wipe off excess glue.

Leave for at least 24 hours to dry.

Assemble the other end in the same manner.

8 Mark a radius on each top corner using a suitable round container (Figure 97). The actual size chosen is a matter of personal preference. Remove as much as possible of this corner with one straight saw cut and surform to the marked curve. Try to keep edges sharp. (See the corner detail illustrated in Figure 97).

At this stage you should remove (using your Surform) any small 'steps' between the spars and the legs which have resulted from imperfect alignment of the joints.

9 The corner blocks (items 5) are fixed to the base spars (items 3) with glue and 50 mm (2 in) No. 8 screws and cup washers. Mark the profile of the corner block at the ends of each base spar (Figure 98 top).

Drill two 4 mm ($\frac{3}{16}$ in) diameter holes on a line along the centre of this strip and 20 mm ($\frac{3}{4}$ in) in from each end (Figure 98).

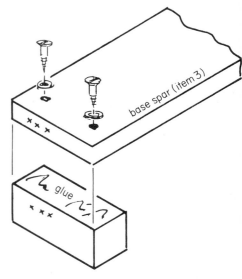

10 Spread glue over the face of the corner block and position the base spar, being very carful to keep the edges (marked *XXX* in Figure 99) flush. Place the screws with their cup washers in the holes. Tap them gently on the head with a hammer to give the threads a bit of bite. Screw home.

Wipe off excess glue.

Repeat for each corner block.

Spot the deliberate error in the spar assembly shown inset in Figure 100 and ensure that you do not make the same mistake!

In order to give the base a slight slope from front to back, the ledge (item 4) is higher on the front base spar than it is on the back base spar.

Figure 99 Fixing the corner block into position

11 First fix the ledge on the front base spare.

Mark a line (*AB* in Figure 101) one slat's width from the top of the spar. Six or seven 37 mm (1$\frac{1}{2}$ in) oval brad nails should be evenly spaced along the ledge and hammered in until the tips can just be felt sticking through the other side. Apply glue as shown in Figure 101. Position the spar, and hammer the nails home. Wipe off excess glue. (The spar will not be a tight fit between the corner blocks but this will not matter.)

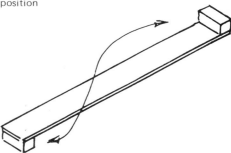

12 The ledge on the back base spar is fixed in a similar manner, but here the bottom of the ledge is flush with the bottom of the spar, (faces *xxx* on Figure 102).

13 Mark the profiles of the base spars and their corner blocks on each end assembly, as shown in Figure 103.

Edge *yyy* should be flush with the front outside edge.

Edge *xxx* should be flush with the back inside edge.

Figure 100 Ensure that both corner blocks are on the same side of the spar — the mistake shown here can happen all too easily!

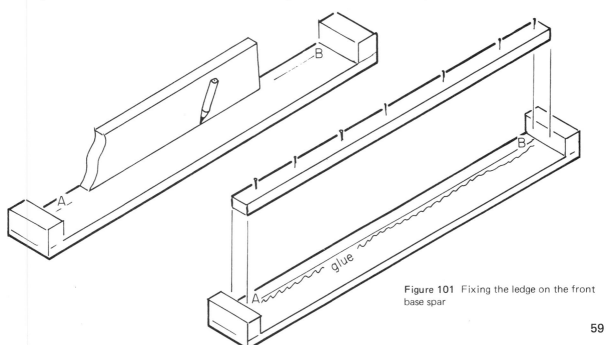

Figure 101 Fixing the ledge on the front base spar

59

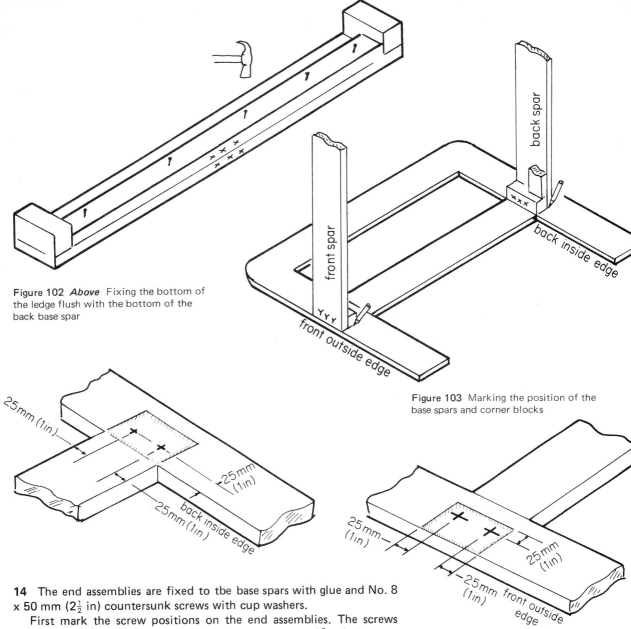

Figure 102 *Above* Fixing the bottom of the ledge flush with the bottom of the back base spar

Figure 103 Marking the position of the base spars and corner blocks

Figure 104 Drilling the positions of the screws to enter the corner blocks

14 The end assemblies are fixed to tbe base spars with glue and No. 8 x 50 mm ($2\frac{1}{2}$ in) countersunk screws with cup washers.

First mark the screw positions on the end assemblies. The screws must enter the corner block, not the spar. Drill 4 mm ($\frac{3}{16}$ in) diameter holes 25 mm (1 in) in from the ends and 25 mm (1 in) from the edges of the corner block part of the profile as shown in Figure 104.

Now glue and screw the base spars into position from the outside.

15 Check that the diagonals are the same length (Figure 105). Fix the two end slats in position with glue and nails (Figure 106). At each end, one 37 mm ($1\frac{1}{2}$ in) oval brad is hammered in vertically, then two are fixed in dovetail fashion (see Nailing, page 14). Leave for 24 hours until the glue has set.

The remaining seven slats should then be positioned with a gap of approximately 50 mm (2 in) between each slat.

The positions of the slats can then be adjusted until the gaps are visually equal.

Mark these positions and fix the spars with glue and three 37 mm ($1\frac{1}{2}$ in) oval brads at each end as described above.

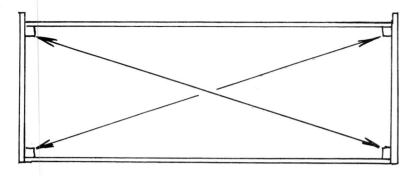

Figure 105 Check that the diagonals are the same length

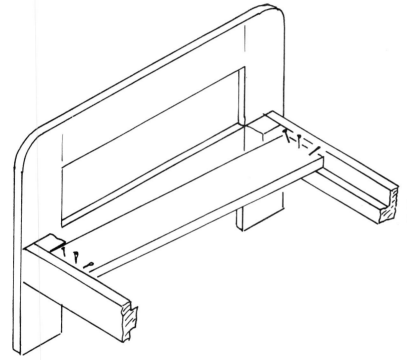

Figure 106 Fixing the end slats in position

16 Aluminium angle bar was suggested for item 8 as this material is relatively easy to drill.

If this was unobtainable and you had to resort to mild steel, you are advised to look around for a heavy-duty power drill to do the drilling. Failing this, make sure that the drill bit is sharp when you start work, and accept the fact that it will probably be very blunt when you have finished.

The holes marked *B* in Figure 107 (top) fix the angle bar to the end assembly, and the holes marked *A* fix the back rest to the angle bar.

The dimensions in Figure 107 (bottom) are similar to those in Figure 107 (top), but the items are mirror images of each other.

Mark the positions as shown in Figure 107 (top). Position a nail point in the centre of each mark and hammer once, to make a small crater. This will serve as a starting point for the drill.

Mark these positions either *A* or *B* and drill each with a 3 mm ($\frac{1}{8}$ in) drill. A few drops of machine oil in the hole being drilled will help to keep the drill bit cool.

Next re-drill each position with a 6 mm ($\frac{1}{4}$ in) drill bit.

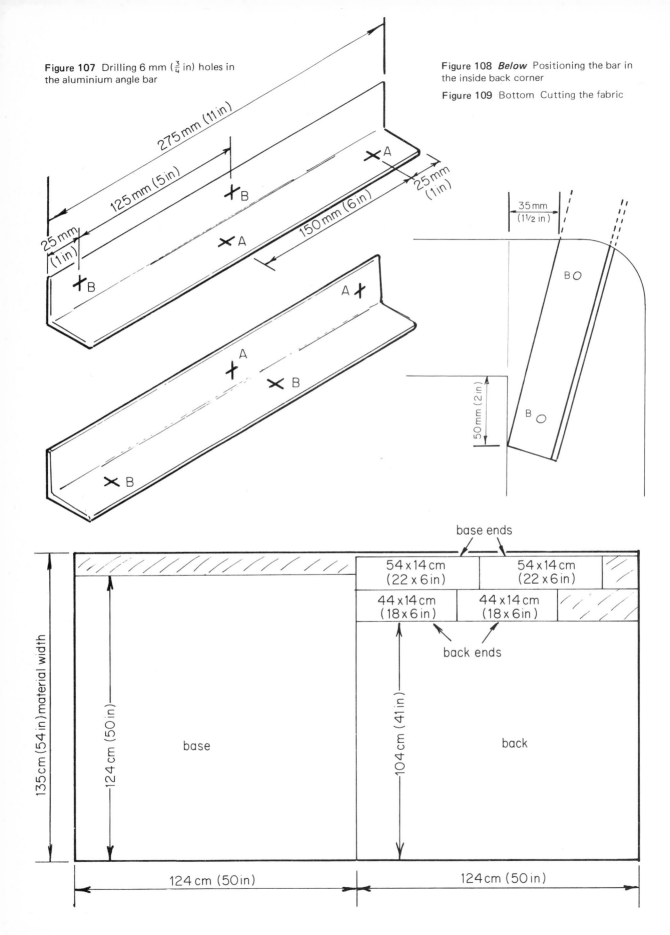

Figure 107 Drilling 6 mm ($\frac{3}{4}$ in) holes in the aluminium angle bar

Figure 108 *Below* Positioning the bar in the inside back corner

Figure 109 Bottom Cutting the fabric

275 mm (11 in)

125 mm (5 in)

25 mm (1 in)

25 mm (1 in)

150 mm (6 in)

25 mm (1 in)

35 mm ($1\frac{1}{2}$ in)

50 mm (2 in)

B

A

base ends

| 54 x 14 cm (22 x 6 in) | 54 x 14 cm (22 x 6 in) |
| 44 x 14 cm (18 x 6 in) | 44 x 14 cm (18 x 6 in) |

back ends

135 cm (54 in) material width

124 cm (50 in)

base

104 cm (41 in)

back

124 cm (50 in)

124 cm (50 in)

If you are using mild steel, it must be painted before assembly. Aluminium alloy may simply be polished.

17 Position the appropriate angle in position in the inside back corner of an end as shown in Figure 108.

Drill through the *B* holes in the angle bar, and through the wood with a 6 mm ($\frac{1}{4}$ in) drill bit.

Bolt the angle bar in position, keeping the nuts on the inside and the slotted round head on the outside.

Fix the other angle bar at the other end in the same manner.

Now fix the back rest (item 7) with 25 mm (1 in) x No. 10 wood screws and cup washers, screwed in from the back. The back rest should protrude about 25 mm (1 in) above the top of the support angles, and the upper edges may be rounded off if desired.

Finish as described in Techniques, page 00.

18 Finally cover the upholstery foam.

The layout to be used for cutting the upholstery fabric is shown in Figure 109.

For the method used to cover the foam refer to Figures 74-6 on page 74.

THREE-SEATER SOFA Project 8

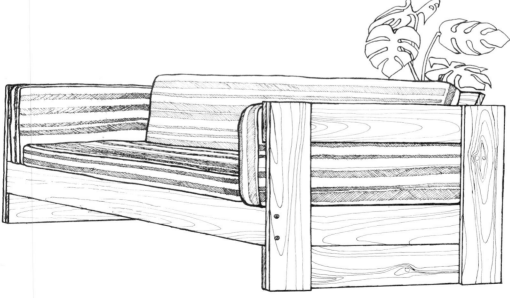

This three-seater sofa is easy to make, light, strong, and attractive. The style can be shortened to armchair width, but the end cushions should not be omitted.

Materials

Item no.	Description	Quantity
1	dressed red pine 145 x 20 x 600 mm (6 in x 1 in nom x 2 ft)	4
2	dressed red pine 145 x 20 x 800 mm (6 in x 1 in nom x 2 ft 8 in)	4
3	dressed red pine 145 x 20 x 750 mm (6 in x 1 in nom x 2 ft 6 in)	2
4	dressed red pine 145 mm x 20 mm x 2 m (6 in x 1 in nom x 6 ft 8 in)	2
5	dressed pine 45 mm x 20 mm x 1.86 m (2 in x 1 in nom x 6 ft 3 in)	2
6	dressed pine 45 x 45 x 145 mm (2 x 2 nom x $5\frac{3}{4}$ in)	6
7	dressed red pine 95 x 20 x 750 mm (4 in x 1 in nom x 2 ft 6 in)	13

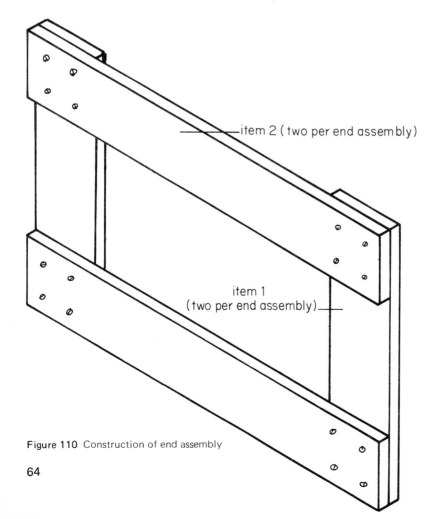

item 2 (two per end assembly)

item 1
(two per end assembly)

Figure 110 Construction of end assembly

64

Item no.	Description		Quantity
8*	dressed red pine 195 mm x 20 mm x 1.96 m (8 in x 1 in nom x 6 ft $6\frac{1}{2}$ in)		1
	35 mm ($1\frac{1}{2}$ in) No. 8 countersunk wood screws		60
	No. 8 cup washers		60
	65 mm ($2\frac{1}{2}$ in) No. 10 countersunk wood screws		4
	No. 10 cup washers		4
	PVA woodworker's adhesive		500 ml (1 pt)
	varnish		as needed
	glass or garnet paper	medium fine	2 sheets 2 sheets
	100 mm (4 in) upholstery foam: base cushion 560 mm x 1.8 m (1 ft 10 in x 6 ft) back cushion 440 mm x 1.8 m (17 in x 6 ft) side cushions 700 x 330 mm (2ft 4 in x 1 ft 1 in)		1 1 2
	fabric (to cover cushions) 135 cm (54 in) wide, 5.20 m ($5\frac{1}{8}$ yd) long		

*The length of this spar ties in fairly critically with the length of item 4 so ask your supplier to be as careful as possible when cutting items 4 and 8.

Method

1 Figure 110 shows a completed end assembly, with screws and cup washers. You may find it useful to refer to this Figure as the building of the end assembly progresses.

2 The screw positions on each end of item 2 (there are two such items on each end assembly) are fixed, using a paper template (see Figure 111). First take a piece of paper 145 mm ($5\frac{3}{4}$ in) square: 145 mm (6 in nom), equals the width of one item 2.

Fold the paper, edge-to-edge, and subsequently fold the folded edge to the open edge.

Open up these folds. Repeat the process with the other edges being folded together. Unfold.

Mark the grid of fold lines at the four positions indicated in Figure 111. These are the four screw positions.

3 Position the template on the end of item 2 and make a pencil mark through the template on to the wood. Drill through each of these positions with a 5 mm ($\frac{3}{16}$ in) drill, onto a piece of waste wood (Figure 112).

There are four such holes drilled in this way at each end of item 2.

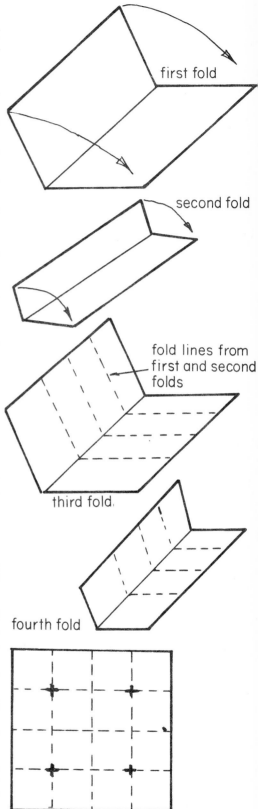

first fold

second fold

fold lines from first and second folds

third fold

fourth fold

Figure 111 Folding a paper template

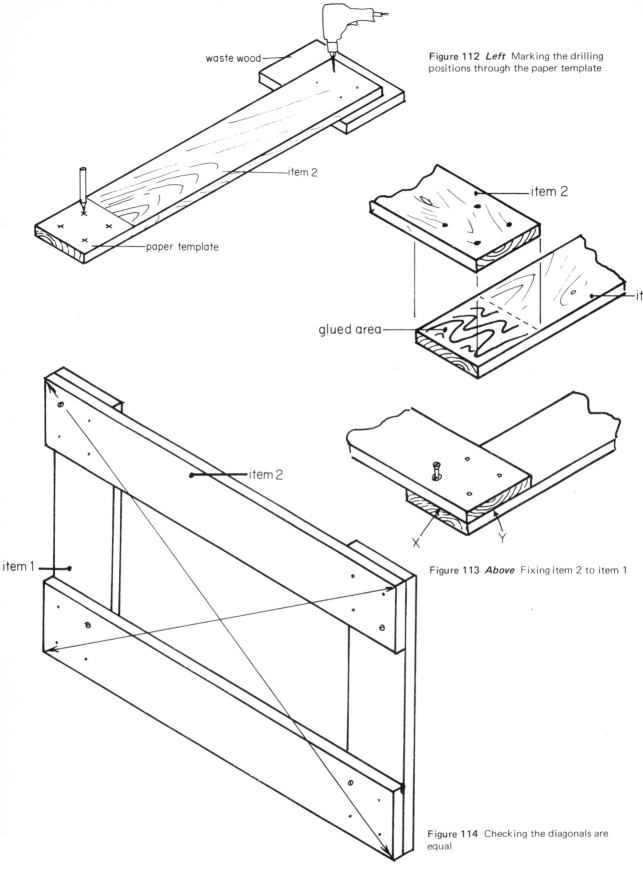

waste wood

Figure 112 *Left* Marking the drilling positions through the paper template

item 2

paper template

item 2

glued area

ite

item 2

item 1

X   Y

Figure 113 *Above* Fixing item 2 to item 1

Figure 114 Checking the diagonals are equal

66

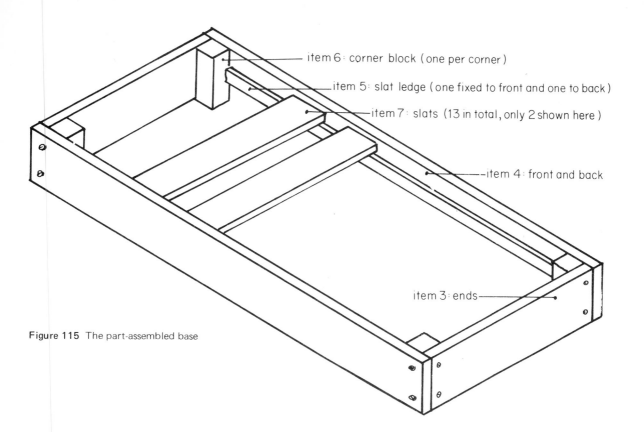

item 6: corner block (one per corner)

item 5: slat ledge (one fixed to front and one to back)

item 7: slats (13 in total, only 2 shown here)

item 4: front and back

item 3: ends

Figure 115 The part-assembled base

4 Position the corner of item 2 over the corner of item 1 and mark the position of the corner on item 1.

Apply glue liberally as shown in Figure 113. Position item 2, making sure that the edges marked *x* and *y* in Figure 113 are flush.

Half hammer — half screw (see Screwing, page 15) one screw with its cup washer into any one of the four screw positions.

Repeat for all four corners of the end assembly — one screw per corner.

5 The diagonals on the end assembly must now be checked to ensure that they are equal to within about 6 mm ($\frac{1}{4}$ in) (Figure 114).

If the assembly is reluctant to change to the correct shape, even after a degree of physical persuasion, slacken off each screw slightly and try again.

Now half hammer, half screw each of the remaining three screws and cup washers per corner.

Repeat operations 3 to 5 for the other end assembly.

6 Figure 115 shows the part-assembled base with item numbers. You should refer to this figure as the assemble of the base progresses.

7 The screw fixing holes in the front, back, and ends of the base assembly (items 3 and 4) are positioned by means of a paper template made as shown in Figure 116.

Take a strip of paper the same width as items 3 and 4 — 145 mm (6 in nom). The length of the strip is important. Place item 6 at the end of this strip and mark its position.

Fold the edge of the paper on to this panel line. Unfold.

Fold each corner on to the pencil line. Unfold.

Mark the drilling positions as indicated in Figure 116.

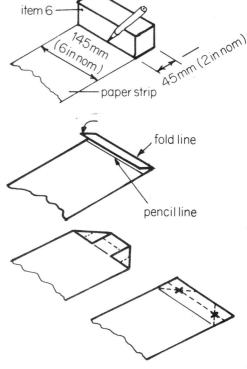

item 6

145mm (6in nom)

45mm (2 in nom)

paper strip

fold line

pencil line

Figure 116 Making a paper template for the drill hole positions

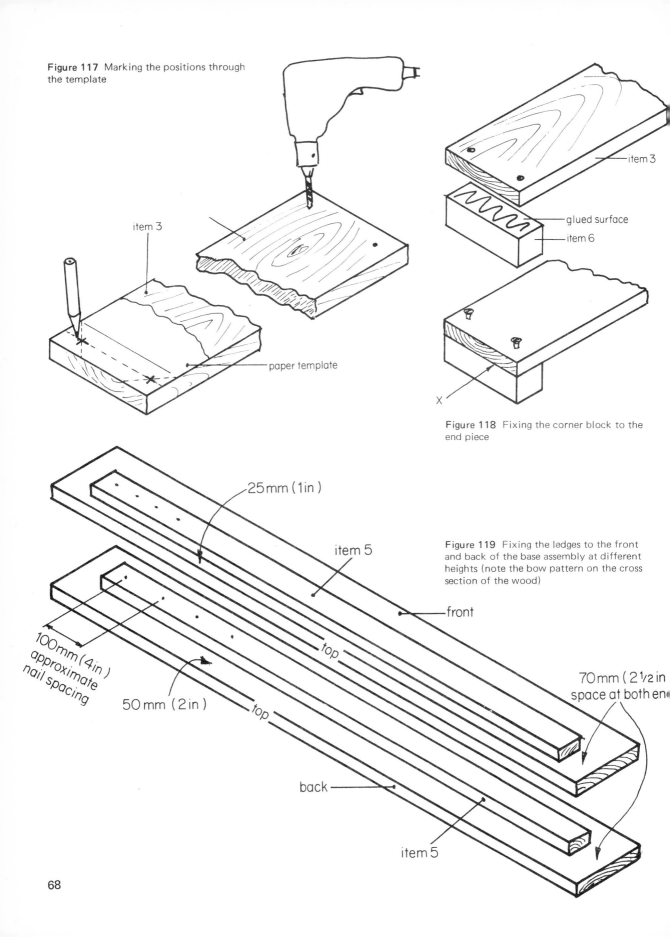

Figure 117 Marking the positions through the template

item 3

paper template

item 3

item 3

glued surface

item 6

X

Figure 118 Fixing the corner block to the end piece

25mm (1in)

item 5

Figure 119 Fixing the ledges to the front and back of the base assembly at different heights (note the bow pattern on the cross section of the wood)

front

100mm (4in)
approximate
nail spacing

top

50mm (2in)

top

70mm (2½in
space at both end

back

item 5

8 Two 4.5 mm ($\frac{3}{16}$ in) diameter holes are now drilled at each end of item 3 (labelled 'ends' in Figure 115).

Place the paper template as shown in Figure 117 and mark the hole positions through the template. Drill through. Remember to use a piece of waste wood to protect your work surface. Countersink each hole with the largest drill available (see Drilling, page 18).

9 Apply glue to item 6 as shown in Figure 118. Position item 3 on item 6.

Half hammer, half screw two 37 mm ($1\frac{1}{3}$ in) No. 8 screws into position as indicated in Figure 118 ensuring that the edge marked *X* is flush.

Do not use cup washers. The screw heads can be screwed below the surface because of the countersinking on each hole.

Repeat, fixing a corner block (item 6) to each end of item 3.

Set aside for at least 12 hours to allow the glue to set.

10 In order to give a slight downwards slope from the front to the back, the ledges (item 5) on which the seating spars rest, are fixed to the front and back of the base assembly (item 4) at different heights.

Item 5 should be at least 70 mm ($2\frac{1}{2}$ in) shorter than item 4 at each end, a total of 140 mm (5 in) shorter. Check this before proceeding and cut item 5 if necessary.

Refer to Figure 119. Mark lightly in pencil the top edge of items 4. Place the ledges (items 5) on items 4 as shown and mark their positions in pencil.

The ledges are held in place with glue and 37 mm ($1\frac{1}{2}$ in) oval brads spaced at approximately 100 mm (4 in) intervals.

First hammer all the nails into the ledges until the tips just protrude through the other side.

Apply glue to the underside of the ledges and place them in the pre-marked positions. The nail tips should stop the ledges sliding about on the wet glue.

Hammer the nails home.

Wipe off excess glue.

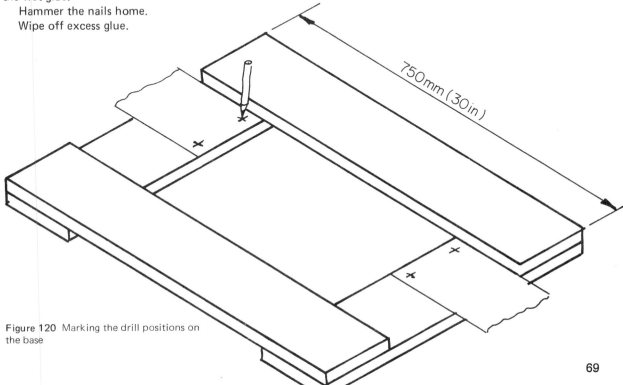

Figure 120 Marking the drill positions on the base

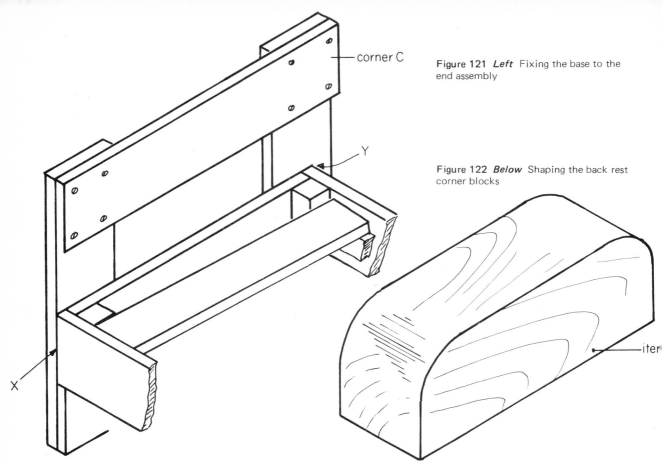

corner C

X

Y

iter

Figure 121 *Left* Fixing the base to the end assembly

Figure 122 *Below* Shaping the back rest corner blocks

11 Mark the front and back (see Figure 120) in four positions (two at each end) using the paper template shown.

Drill 4.5 mm ($\frac{3}{16}$ in) clearance holes in each of these positions: 4 holes in the front, 4 holes in the back. Now glue and screw items 4 to the ends (items 3) with 37 mm ($1\frac{1}{2}$ in) No. 8 screws and cup washers. Use half hammer, half screw method (see Screwing, page 15).

12 Now fix the slats (item 8) to the base assembly. Without glue, position the eleven slats on the ledges and, judging by eye, adjust them until the spaces are even. The two end slats should be fixed against the corner blocks. The home carpenter will undoubtedly receive lots of unsolicited advice on an operation like this. Ignore It!

Mark the positions and remove the slats. Apply a good squirt of PVA adhesive to the ledge on each slat position and firmly push the slat into place. Repeat for all the slats.

Wipe off excess glue and lay aside for at least half-an-hour before handling the base assembly — gently as yet.

13 Next fix the base assembly to the end assembly. Using the paper template that you made to fix the hole positions on the base (Figure 120), mark the positions of four 5 mm ($\frac{3}{16}$ in) holes on each end assembly. Drill through these markings. Remember to place a piece of waste wood underneath.

14 Glue and half hammer, half screw the base assembly to the end assemblies from the outside through these holes with 35 mm ($1\frac{1}{2}$ in) No. 8 screws and cup washers.

Note: The base assembly fits flush at the front *x* but not at the back (Figure 121). So do not panic!

70

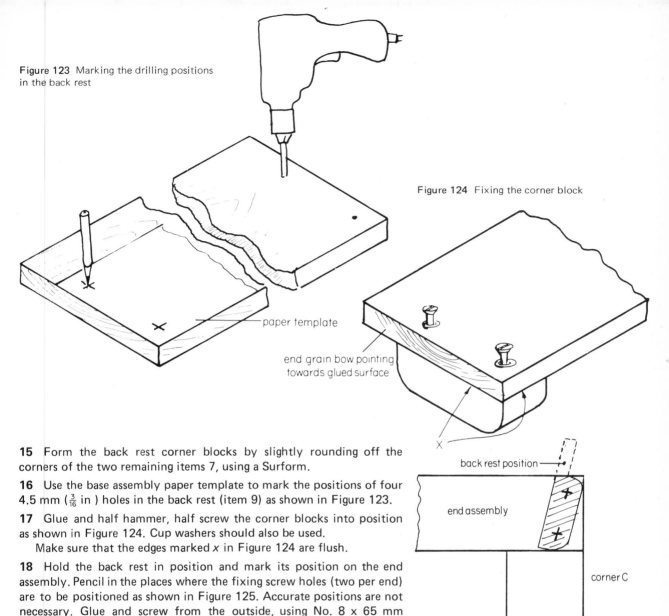

Figure 123 Marking the drilling positions in the back rest

Figure 124 Fixing the corner block

paper template

end grain bow pointing towards glued surface

back rest position

end assembly

corner C

15 Form the back rest corner blocks by slightly rounding off the corners of the two remaining items 7, using a Surform.

16 Use the base assembly paper template to mark the positions of four 4.5 mm ($\frac{3}{16}$ in) holes in the back rest (item 9) as shown in Figure 123.

17 Glue and half hammer, half screw the corner blocks into position as shown in Figure 124. Cup washers should also be used.
Make sure that the edges marked *x* in Figure 124 are flush.

18 Hold the back rest in position and mark its position on the end assembly. Pencil in the places where the fixing screw holes (two per end) are to be positioned as shown in Figure 125. Accurate positions are not necessary. Glue and screw from the outside, using No. 8 x 65 mm ($2\frac{1}{2}$ in) screws and cup washers.

Figure 125 *Above* Marking the screw positions in the end assembly

Figure 126 Cutting out the fabric

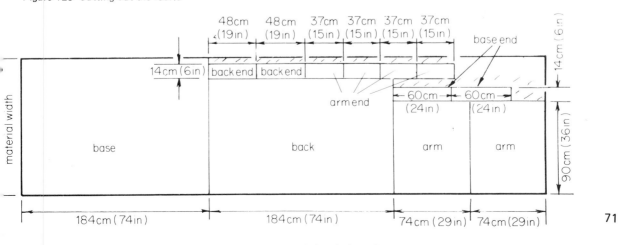

material width

| 48cm (19in) | 48cm (19in) | 37cm (15in) | 37cm (15in) | 37cm (15in) | 37cm (15in) | 14cm (6in) |

14cm (6in) | back end | back end

arm end | base end

60cm (24in) | 60cm (24in)

90cm (36in)

base | back | arm | arm

184cm (74in) | 184cm (74in) | 74cm (29in) | 74cm (29in)

material length 5.2m (5¼yd)

71

Note: The back rest may be either loose or a fairly tight fit. If it is a bit on the loose side, or if the back rest is too long to fit into the space, loosen off very slightly the screw inserted in operation 14.

Varnish finish as described in Finishing, page 21, and upholster the cushions.

The settee can be lengthened or, of course, reduced to armchair width. The required modifications to the plans will now be obvious.

For cutting layout for fabric see Figure 126. Cover each piece of foam as described on page 74.

Project 9
DINING TABLE

The table described here is traditional in style, if not in design.

Like all items of household furniture, which utilise good materials and are carefully finished, it is both special and at the same time 'everyday'.

Used without a tablecloth, little Johnny's tomato ketchup stains will come off with a wipe, but for those special, candle-lit dinners you will find that the pine surface is beautifully complemented by table-mats in unbleached linen, woven rush, or woven split cane. Do be careful not to hide too much of your loving handiwork, as you might slow down the flow of admiring compliments!

Materials

Item no.	Description		Quantity
1*	red pine 95 mm x 37 mm x 1.25 m (4 in x 1½ in nom x 4 ft 6 in)		7
2	red pine 120 mm x 45 mm x 1.25 m (5 in x 2 in nom x 4 ft 6 in)		2
3	pine 70 x 45 x 660 mm (3 in x 2 in nom x 2 ft 3 in)		3
4	red pine 70 x 70 x 700 mm (3 in x 3 in nom x 2 ft 3 in)		4
5	box-head wire nails 100 mm (4 in)		20
6	50 mm (2 in) oval brads		10
7	37 mm (1½ in) oval brads		20
8†	'one shot' waterproof wood glue		200 ml (½ pt) approx
9	65 mm (2½ in) x NO. 10 countersunk screws		8
10	No. 10 cup washers (if available)		4
	glass or garnet paper	heavy medium light	2 sheets 2 sheets 2 sheets
	silk or gloss varnish		

*If the recommended section is not available, 95 mm x 45 mm (4 in x 2 in nom) may be used, although this will, of course, increase the weight.

†This is used for its strength and not for its water-resistant properties.

Method

1 First mark the positions of the bracing spars (item 3) on the top slats (item 1) (Figure 128).

Working on a flat surface, stack the seven top slats together, narrow edges upwards. They will not be exactly the same length, but to cut the finishing work to a minimum, make sure that they are flush at one end of this stack e.g. end *A*, in Figure 128. Do not trust your eye alone for this operation, check it with your square.

Mark firm pencil lines across the stack as shown in Figure 128, i.e. 200 mm (8 in) from each end, and approximately in the centre. All these lines should be at 90° to the edge of the stack. Use your square to ensure accuracy in this respect.

Mark a numbering sequence 1-7, as shown in Figure 128, and lay the slats in this order.

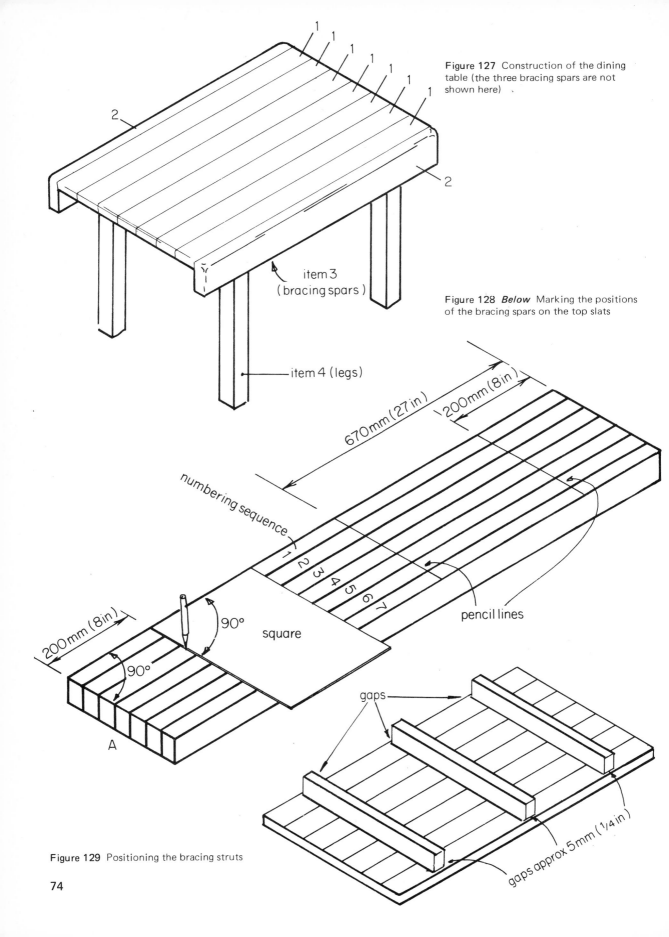

Figure 127 Construction of the dining table (the three bracing spars are not shown here)

1

1

1

2

2

item 3 (bracing spars)

item 4 (legs)

Figure 128 *Below* Marking the positions of the bracing spars on the top slats

670mm (27 in)

200mm (8in)

numbering sequence

1 2 3 4 5 6 7

pencil lines

200mm (8in)

90°

90°

square

A

gaps

gaps approx 5mm (1/4 in)

Figure 129 Positioning the bracing struts

2 Lay the top slats (item 1) out on a flat surface, and place the bracing struts (items 3) in position on top (Figure 129).

There should be a gap of about 5 mm ($\frac{1}{4}$ in) at either end of the bracing struts.

If the bracing struts stick out beyond the top slats, they must be shortened to the required length, either by sawing or surforming.

Do not worry too much if the gap exceeds 5 mm ($\frac{1}{4}$ in) as it will be hidden by the legs in the finished table.

3 Now proceed to fix the first slat.

The slat to be fixed (slat 1) and slat 7 are placed in the positions shown in Figure 130. Slat 7 is only used here to ensure that the bracing struts (item 3) remain parallel throughout the fixing operation.

Ensure that the pencil lines line-up with the edges of the spars (the centre one is not quite so important) and mark with a pencil the positions of the three 50 mm (2 in) oval brads so that they will fix the slat to the bracing struts.

Remove slat 1 from the struts and hammer the three brads into position until the nail points just protrude from the bottom of the slat.

Apply glue to the struts where they will be fixed to slat 1 and position the slat on the struts.

Do the pencil lines on the slat still *exactly* match the edge of the struts?

Is the small gap discussed in operation 2 still the right size?

Keep slat 7 in position during this operation.

Once you are satisfied that all is well, hammer the nails fully home (try not to damage the table surface) and then punch them below the surface.

4 Keep slat 7 in the position shown in Figure 130 until operation 4 is complete.

A single vertical nail will probably not provide a strong enough fixing to compress the glue. It is therefore necessary to fix the top slat with a pair of 50 mm (2 in) brads in dovetail fashion as shown in Figure 131.

Figure 130 Fixing the first slat — note the positioning of the pencil lines

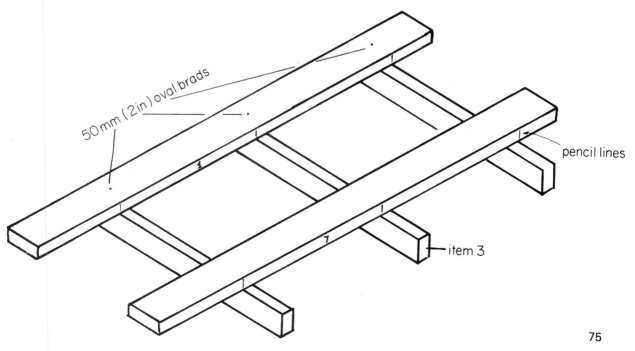

50 mm (2 in) oval brads

pencil lines

item 3

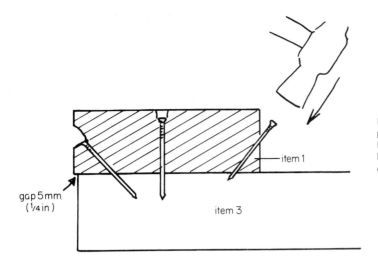

gap 5mm
(¼ in)

item 1

item 3

Figure 131 The dovetail nails can be punched below the surface or simply hammered below (as shown on the left) — be careful however to keep the outer corners sharp

If you have any trouble starting the nail off at an angle, drive it into the wood straight until the point is in, and then simply twist it round to the correct angle and complete the operation (Figure 132).

The project should now be left for 3-4 hours to allow the glue to partially set. This will reduce the risk of movement during subsequent stages.

5 Hammer three 37 mm (1½ in) oval brad nails half-way into the edge of this first slat in the region of the three bracing struts. Keep them as horizontal as possible. The heads should stick out about 10-15 mm (½ in) (see Figure 133).

These nails are to be used as location pins for slat 2. Spread glue fairly liberally on to the surfaces that will be in contact with slat 2.

6 Place slat 2 in position on the bracing struts, resting against the sticking-out nails.

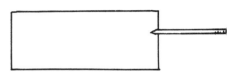

Figure 132 Starting the nail straight and twisting it to the correct angle

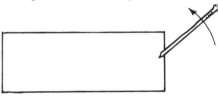

Figure 133 Positioning the location pins

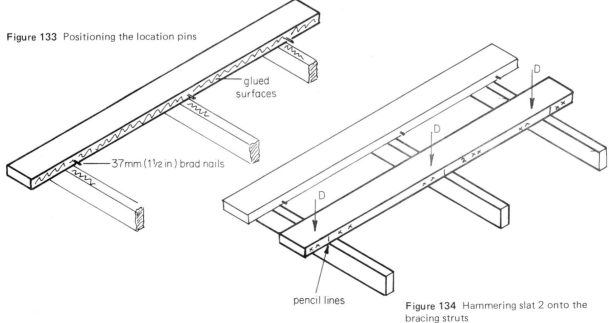

glued surfaces

37mm (1½ in) brad nails

pencil lines

Figure 134 Hammering slat 2 onto the bracing struts

Carefully ensure that the pencil marks on the top slats match up with the edges of the bracing struts. The next stage is best done with the help of a friend.

A piece of waste wood is rested against surface *xxx* (Starting at either end) and while your helper pushes down firmly in direction *D*, you hammer against the waste wood until the edges of the slats come into contact (Figure 134). Repeat this for the other two positions.

7 The slat is now fixed firmly into place by using 100 mm (4 in) wire nails, driven in at an angle through the slat and the bracing strut (Figure 135). There will be three nails per slat.

The nails should be hammered below the surface.

Great care must be taken to avoid damaging the upper edge of the slat. However, if some damage is inflicted, do not attempt any remedial action at this stage. Leave any splintered or crushed wood as it is.

Repeat this operation until all the slats are fixed, wiping off excess glue as you go along.

8 Now proceed to fix the side slats (item 2).

The actual position of the 100 mm (4 in) nails used to fix the side slats is not important although the table looks better if they are at least the same distance from the top surface — 15 mm ($\frac{3}{4}$ in). The finished table is also probably a fraction stronger if the nails are driven in in the vicinity of the underneath bracing struts.

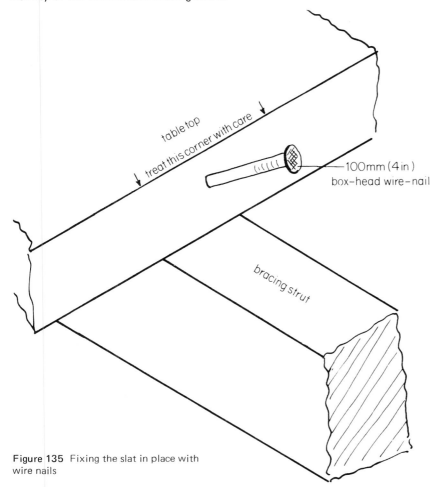

table top

treat this corner with care

100mm (4 in) box-head wire-nail

bracing strut

Figure 135 Fixing the slat in place with wire nails

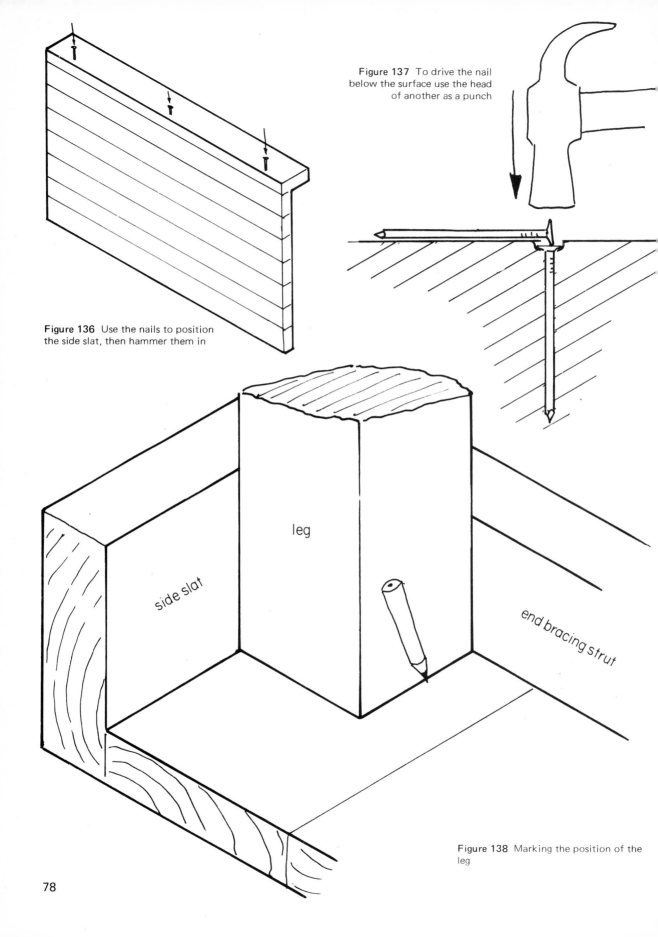

Figure 136 Use the nails to position the side slat, then hammer them in

Figure 137 To drive the nail below the surface use the head of another as a punch

side slat

leg

end bracing strut

Figure 138 Marking the position of the leg

Mark the positions of the nails, and working with the side slats separate from the rest of the assembly, drive in the three nails until the points just protrude through the other side.

Working with the top on its side (Figure 136) apply glue along the edge and position the side slat. The nail tips should give a positive location, preventing any slip up on the wet glue. Make sure that the top surface and the ends are flush, and then hammer the nails fully home.

The nails should be driven below the surface using a 100 mm (4 in) nail on its side and hammering the head of one against the head of the other (see Figure 137).

It is only necessary to use this method of nail-punching when large nails are being used.

Repeat this operation for the second side slat.

9 Before the legs are fixed, the surface should be surformed flat (see Surforming, page 20) and all corners and edges should be rounded off. This should be done with the completed top resting firmly on the floor. Although there is no real problem here regarding skill it is, without a doubt, hard physical work. Be prepared for about 2 hours labour *before* you start thinking about abandoning your Surform and going on to the next stage.

Cream-coloured wood-filler should be pushed firmly into all cracks, nail holes, and dents and allowed to dry. The top can then be smoothed using rough, then medium, then smooth glass or garnet paper until the surface feels good to the touch.

10 Figure 138 shows a detail of one corner of the completed top assembly (upside down) with the leg in position. Note that the leg is positioned to the outside and not to the inside of the bracing strut.

Mark with a pencil on the inverted top assembly the area occupied by the leg (Figure 138).

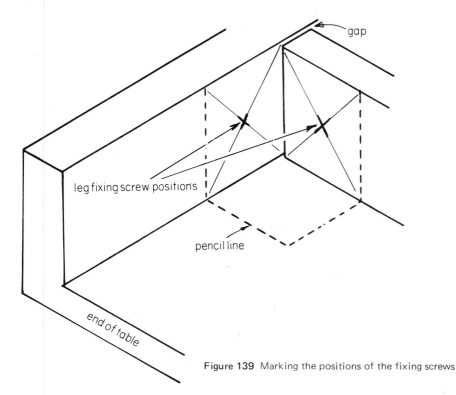

Figure 139 Marking the positions of the fixing screws

Remove the leg. To find the position of the fixing screws, mark the diagonals on the rectangles formed by the leg positions on the side slat and on the bracing strut (Figure 139).

Drill through the side slat and the bracing strut in these positions using a 5 mm ($\frac{3}{16}$ in) diameter drill bit.

Repeat this operation for all four corners.

11 Finally fix the legs.

This is done with the table upside-down and is another job which might benefit from the presence of a friendly hand to hold the leg firmly into the corner while the screws are driven home.

Spread glue liberally on the table area to which the leg is to be fixed and hold the leg firmly into the corner. It should not be ncesssary to use pilot holes or a hammer for the screws, but you will have to push very firmly on the screwdriver until the screw bites.

Position 1 (Figure 140):

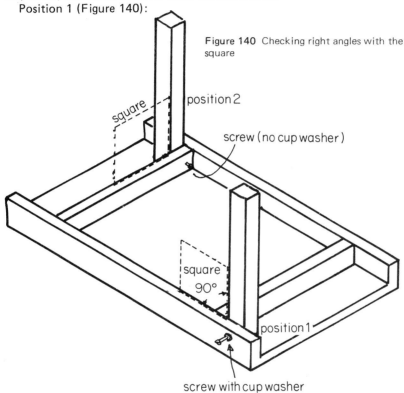

Figure 140 Checking right angles with the square

position 2

square

screw (no cup washer)

square
90°

position 1

screw with cup washer

If No. 10 cup washers are not available you may prefer to use dome-headed screws in these four outside positions.

Just before the screw is fully home, you helper should check that the leg is at right angles to the side spar, by placing the square in the position indicated in figure 112. Only when this angle is correct should the screw be fully tightened.

Position 2 (Figure 140):

This figure shows the position of the square along the bracing strut when the inside screws are being fixed.

The screwing procedure is the same and each leg should be fully fixed with glue and both screws, before going on to the next.

Wipe off excess glue after each fixing operation is complete.

Do not attempt to rest the table on its legs for at least 24 hours by which time the glue should be fully set. It is the glue which supports the table, not the fixing screws.

Leg wobble
With the best will in the world there is always the chance of a wobble in the finished article. This is most easily remedied by building up one leg, or by building up diagonally opposite legs. This is done using 50 mm (2 in) square pieces of scrap plywood or hardboard which can be glued and nailed in position when the correct thickness has been ascertained.

Finish (see Varnishing, page 21).

Project 10
SINGLE BED

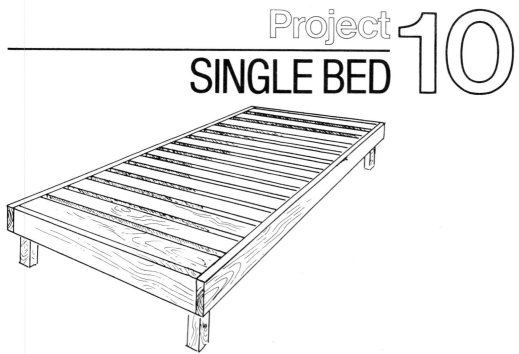

The simple slatted pine bed described here as a single version is used in conjunction with a firm mattress, 3 ft (90 cm) wide and 6 ft 3 in (1.8 m) long. Adjustments should be made if a different mattress size is to be used.

Materials

Item no.	Description	Quantity
1	dressed pine 95 mm x 20 mm x 1.875 m (4 in x 1 in nom x 6 ft 3 in)	2
2	dressed pine 95 x 20 x 850 mm (4 in x 1 in nom x 2 ft 10 in)	14

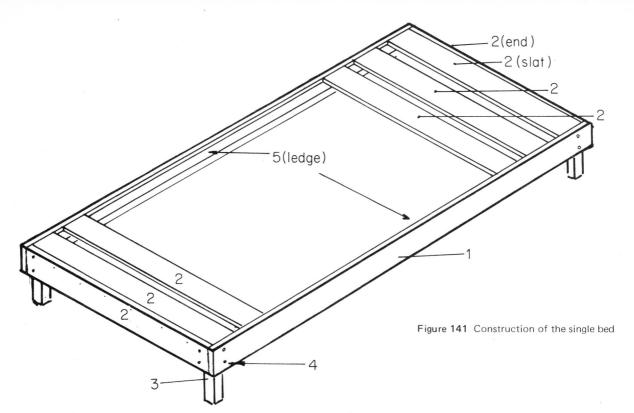

Figure 141 Construction of the single bed

Item no.	Description	Quantity
3	dressed pine 45 x 45 x 300 mm (2 in x 2 in nom x 1 ft)	4
4	37 mm ($1\frac{1}{2}$ in) No. 10 countersunk wood screws and cup washers *or* 37 mm ($1\frac{1}{2}$ in) No. 10 round-head brass screws	16
5	dressed pine 20 mm x 45 mm x 1.8 m (1 in x 2 in nom x 6 ft)	2
6	37 mm ($1\frac{1}{2}$ in) oval brad nails	100 approx
7	PVA woodworker's adhesive	200 ml ($\frac{1}{2}$ pt)

The ends and the slats (items 2) are all supposed to be the same length — at least, when you order them from your supplier that is what you ask for. It is highly unlikely that this is what you will receive, but it is important that each end is as nearly as possible equal to the slat with which it butts (Figure 141).

Method

Pick out two such pairs of item 2 now.

In each pair, one will be treated as a slat and the other as an end.

Complete operations 1-3 on one pair before going on to the next.

1 The slat lies on top of the leg and the position of the slat and of the two legs should now be marked lightly in pencil on the end (Figure 142).

The side with the markings will eventually be the outside of the end.

2 The slat and the end are joined using 37 mm ($1\frac{1}{2}$ in) oval brad nails and glue.

First, two nails are hammered vertically into the centre of the strip which was drawn in Figure 142.

The actual position of the nails along that strip is not important — say a quarter in from either end. The nails should be hammered in until the points just protrude through the timber.

Apply glue to the edge of the slat and bring the two pieces into contact (Figure 143).

Ensure that the edges marked with *x* in Figure 143 are flush.

Hammer the two nails home.

If the joint is closing easily, hammer in another three nails vertically, spacing them evenly, but if there is the slightest sign of warping you will have to use about six nails in dovetail fashion as shown in Figure 143.

Punch these nails below the surface (see Nailing, page 14). Wipe off excess glue.

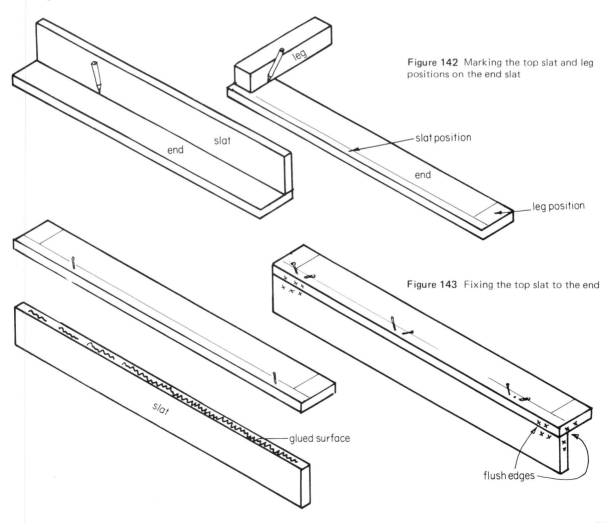

leg

Figure 142 Marking the top slat and leg positions on the end slat

slat position

end

end

slat

leg position

Figure 143 Fixing the top slat to the end

slat

glued surface

flush edges

83

3 Now mark the screwing positions on the end.

Using the thickness of any slat (item 2) as a guide, mark a line across the end holding the slat against the outside edge as shown in Figure 144.

Next, mark two lines, first by holding the slat against edge *x* and then by holding it against line *y* (Figure 144).

The end is drilled through the points where these lines cross, with a 4.5 mm ($\frac{3}{16}$ in) drill. (Remember to use a piece of waste wood as shown in Figure 144).

4 Working on the edge of a table or bench, apply glue fairly liberally to the leg as shown in Figure 145.

Position the leg as shown in Figure 145. Make sure that the edges marked with X are flush and that the angle marked 90° in the figure is indeed a right-angle. Use your square to check this.

Half hammer, half screw (see Screwing, page 15) *one* of the 37 mm ($1\frac{1}{2}$ in) No. 10 screws home, remembering the cup washer if a counter-sunk screw is being used.

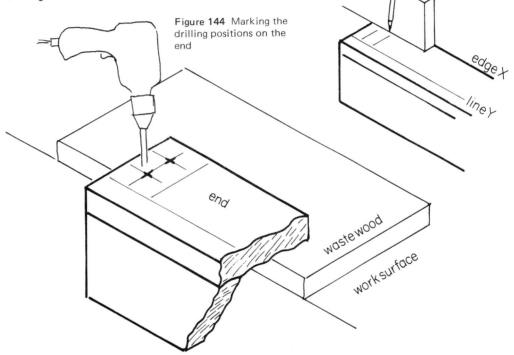

Figure 144 Marking the drilling positions on the end

Figure 145 Fixing the leg with glue and screws

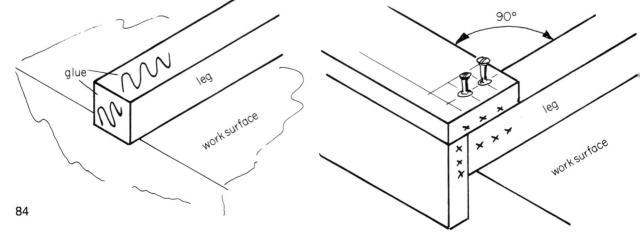

84

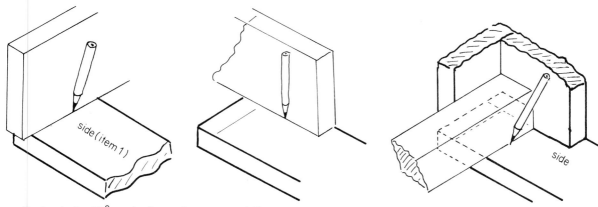

Recheck the 90° angle. It can be corrected if necessary and the other screw can then be inserted in the same way as the first one.

The other slat/end/leg assembly can now be constructed in the same manner.

Figure 146 Marking the position of the leg on the side

5 Now mark the position of the leg on the side (item 1).

Take an unused slat, and, holding it as in Figure 146 mark its position on the side.

Position the whole end/leg assembly on the side and mark the leg position as indicated in Figure 146.

6 Using the slat width as a guide, as before, mark lines x, y, and z by placing the slat edge against line *A*, line *B*, and the edge respectively (Figure 147). This gives you the screw clearance hole positions on the side (marked with crosses in Figure 147).

Figure 147 shows the drilling operation at both ends of the side (item 1).

Use a 4.5 mm ($\frac{3}{16}$ in) diameter drill as before, drilling through on to waste wood.

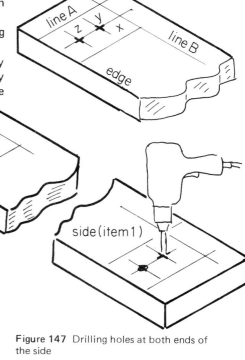

7 Now fix the sides.

These items are fairly long and it would be best to ask a helper to support them during this stage of the work.

Apply glue to all the faces that will be in contact and place the side in position, with the end resting on the floor (Figure 148).

Figure 147 Drilling holes at both ends of the side

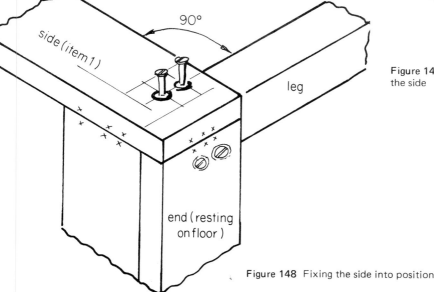

Figure 148 Fixing the side into position

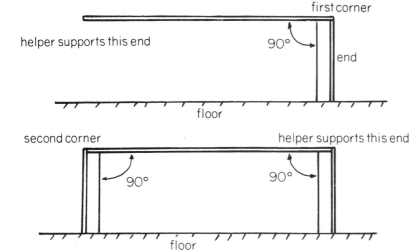

first corner

helper supports this end

90°

end

floor

second corner

helper supports this end

90°

90°

floor

Figure 149 Supporting the side while the first and second corners are glued and screwed into position

Make sure that the edges marked *x* in the figure are flush and that the angle marked 90° is fairly accurate. (Use your square to check this.)

37 mm ($1\frac{1}{2}$ in) No. 10 screws are used with cup washers (or dome-headed screws with no cup washers) for the fixing operation. Drive one screw fully home. Do not half hammer, half screw, as the hammer might strain the glued joint between the leg and the end.

Now check that the angle marked 90° is accurate and adjust if necessary.

Drive home the second screw.

Wipe off excess glue.

8 Fix the corner at the opposite end of the side in a similar manner. (See Figure 149).)

Check that the 90° angles are accurate using your square. If they are out by more than say 35 mm ($1\frac{1}{2}$ in) at the ends, lay the job flat on the floor and adjust the angle (only a fairly small push should be required). Lay some heavy object across the corner to hold it in that position until the glue sets.

Fix the other side (item 1) in the same way.

9 The slats which support the mattress rest on a ledge (item 5), the position and length of which should now be fixed.

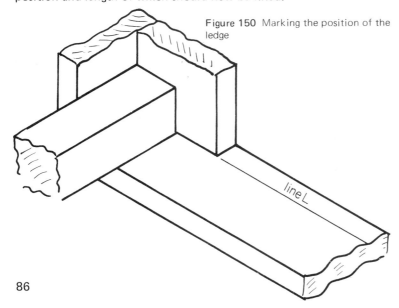

Figure 150 Marking the position of the ledge

line L

Since the slats, when in position, are flush with the top of the bed, the top of the ledge (line L in Figure 150) should be one slat's width from the upper edge.

Mark this line in pencil using a slat held against the top edge, as a guide.

The ledge fits between the legs, but since the ends of the ledge, when in position, will be hidden by the first slat, cut the ledge about 5 mm ($\frac{1}{4}$ in) shorter than the maximum ledge length shown in Figure 151. If you have a bench hook, use it (see Tools, page 11).

10 The ledge must now be fixed.

It is glued, placed in position along line L (see Figure 150), and then nailed using 37 mm ($1\frac{1}{2}$ in) oval brads in the following way.

Fix the position of the ledge with three nails evenly spaced and hammered in vertically along its length.

Eight nails should then be hammered in, in dovetail pairs, again evenly spaced along the length of the ledge (see Nailing, page 14).

Punch nail heads below the surface.

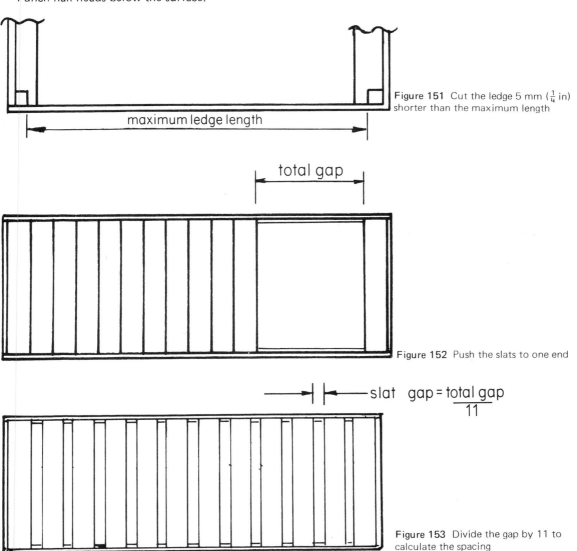

maximum ledge length

Figure 151 Cut the ledge 5 mm ($\frac{1}{4}$ in) shorter than the maximum length

total gap

Figure 152 Push the slats to one end

slat gap = $\dfrac{\text{total gap}}{11}$

Figure 153 Divide the gap by 11 to calculate the spacing

11 The slats are now positioned as follows.

The bed has twelve top slats altogether (item 2), including the two end slats. There are therefore eleven gaps between the slats. To work out the gap between each slat, divide the total gap by eleven.

Place all the slats on the bed and push them all up to one end (Figure 152).

Measure the total gap.

Divide this number by eleven.

Now place the slats in position (Figure 153) and mark on the ledge the exact place occupied by each slat as shown in Figure 154.

Alternative method

This second method is much more in line with the principles of family carpentry.

Lay the slats out along the ledges, and shift them about until they *look* right! Mark these positions.

12 Remove the slats, and one at a time, apply glue on the ledge where it will be in contact with the slat. (Remember to glue both ends.) Replace the slat, lining it up with the positioning marks.

Hammer in one vertical 37 mm ($1\frac{1}{2}$ in) oval brad at each end (the centre nail in Figure 154) and then two nails per end in dovetail fashion.

Purch these nails below the surface.

Repeat until all the slats are fixed, wiping off excess glue as you progress.

13 Finish and varnish (see Finishing, page 20).

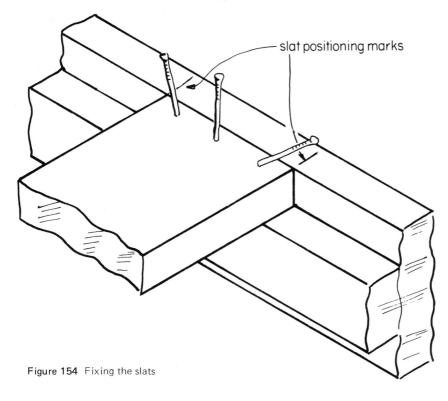

slat positioning marks

Figure 154 Fixing the slats

DOUBLE BED 11

This double bed is almost identical in design to the single bed in the previous project, and so construction details can be taken from that project. There are, however, some changes to the materials required (see Figure 155):

Central spine: dressed pine 20 mm x 95 mm x 1.830 m
(1 in x 4 in nom x 6 ft 1$\frac{1}{4}$ in)

Slats and end (item 2): These should be increased in length and, assuming a mattress width of 1.35 m (4 ft 6 in), you will require fourteen pieces of dressed pine
20 mm x 95 mm x 1.3 m (1 in x 4 in nom x 4 ft 4 in)

Twelve 37 mm (1$\frac{1}{2}$ in) x No. 10 countersunk wood screws and cup washers

A firm mattress, either of the orthopaedic type or of heavier grade upholstery foam at least 100 mm (4 in) thick is required.

Why a central spine? The 20 mm x 95 mm (1 in x 4 in) section slats are fine as they stand for a single bed, since timber of this section only 850 mm (2 ft 10 in) long can easily support the weight of an adult. The increase in length of these slats on the double bed, however, would

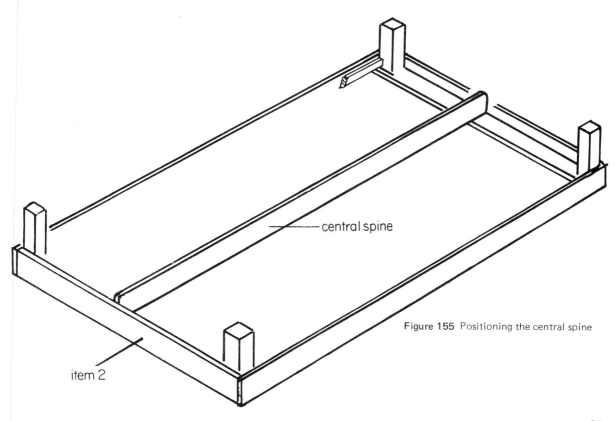

central spine

item 2

Figure 155 Positioning the central spine

89

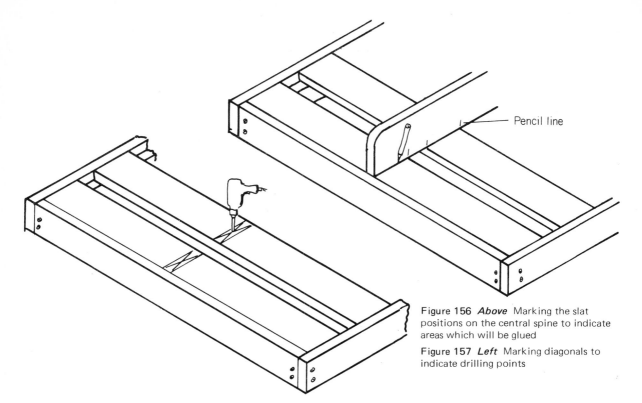

Pencil line

Figure 156 *Above* Marking the slat positions on the central spine to indicate areas which will be glued

Figure 157 *Left* Marking diagonals to indicate drilling points

make it quite possible for a heavier-than-average adult to break the slat by standing at the centre. To save the extra expense of making the slat thicker, a central spine is added.

The central spine makes it unlikely that one slat will take a disproportionate load since the spine shares the force among the bordering slats.

Note that in Figure 155 the spine is shown with rounded ends.

Because the spine rests on the slats, it will protrude below the bottom of the bed. A curve or a chamfer allows this item to blend visually. (See Figure 161 in the following project, Headboards.)

Method

1 The spine is fixed to the slats by screws and glue, and the positions of the screw clearance holes in the slats should now be fixed.

With the bed the correct way up, position the spine as shown in Figure 156, and lightly mark the positon of each side of the spine on each slat. At the same time, mark the slat positions on the spine so that glue may be easily applied to the contact areas later.

Mark diagonals on the spine positions and, at the diagonal crossing points, drill a 4.5 mm ($\frac{3}{16}$ in) diameter hole through each slat (Figure 157).

2 Fitting the central spine is almost certainly a two-man job.

Working with the bed on its end (Figure 158) apply glue to the spine at the slat marks made in operation 1. With your helper holding the spine in position and supporting the bed, drive home the screws with their cup washers in position, fixing the end positions first of all, and working towards the centre. Wipe off excess glue.

Do not try the bed out for 24 hours as the joints may be strained if the bed is used before the glue has fully set.

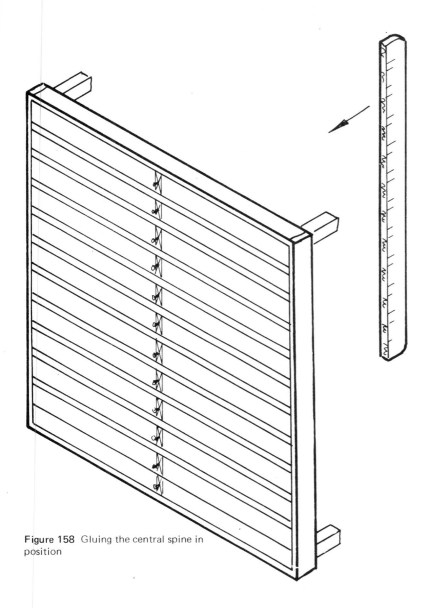

Figure 158 Gluing the central spine in position

Project 12
HEADBOARDS

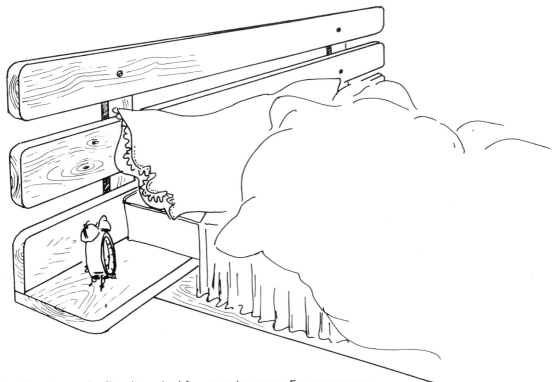

A headboard may be fitted to a bed for several reasons. For appearance (or rather convention); to stop the pillow falling off; or to act as a piece of bedroom furniture in its own right, having shelving incorporated into its design.

Two designs are given here: Style A and Style B. The first is of the very simplest type, the second has a lower shelf fitted.

I do not for a second suggest that these are the only possible types and this is an excellent opportunity to 'customise' your bedroom by designing your own headboard. Some design suggestions are given in Figure 161.

Materials

Item no. Style A	Description	Quantity
1	dressed pine 95 mm x 20 mm x 1.35 m (4 in x 1 in nom x 4 ft 6 in)	2
2	dressed pine 95 x 20 x 500 mm (4 in x 1 in nom x 1 ft 8 in)	2

Item no.	Description	Quantity
3	30 mm ($1\frac{1}{4}$ in) x No. 10 roundhead brass screws *or* 37 mm ($1\frac{1}{2}$ in) x No. 10 countersunk screws (brass or steel) with cup washers	4
	PVA woodworker's adhesive	
	garnet or glass paper medium	1 sheet
	varnish	
Style B		
1	dressed pine 95 mm x 20 mm x 1.950 m (4 in x 1 in nom x 6 ft 6 in)	3
2	dressed pine 145 mm x 20 mm x 1.95 m (6 in x 1 in nom x 6 ft 6 in)	1
3	dressed pine 95 mm x 20 mm x 600 mm (4 in x 1 in nom x 2 ft)	2
4	30 mm ($1\frac{1}{4}$ in) x No. 10 roundhead brass screws *or* 37 mm ($1\frac{1}{2}$ in) x No. 10 countersunk screws (brass or steel with cup washers)	6
	37 mm ($1\frac{1}{2}$ in) oval brad nails	12
	PVA woodworker's adhesive	
	garnet or glass paper medium	1 sheet
	varnish	

style A

style B

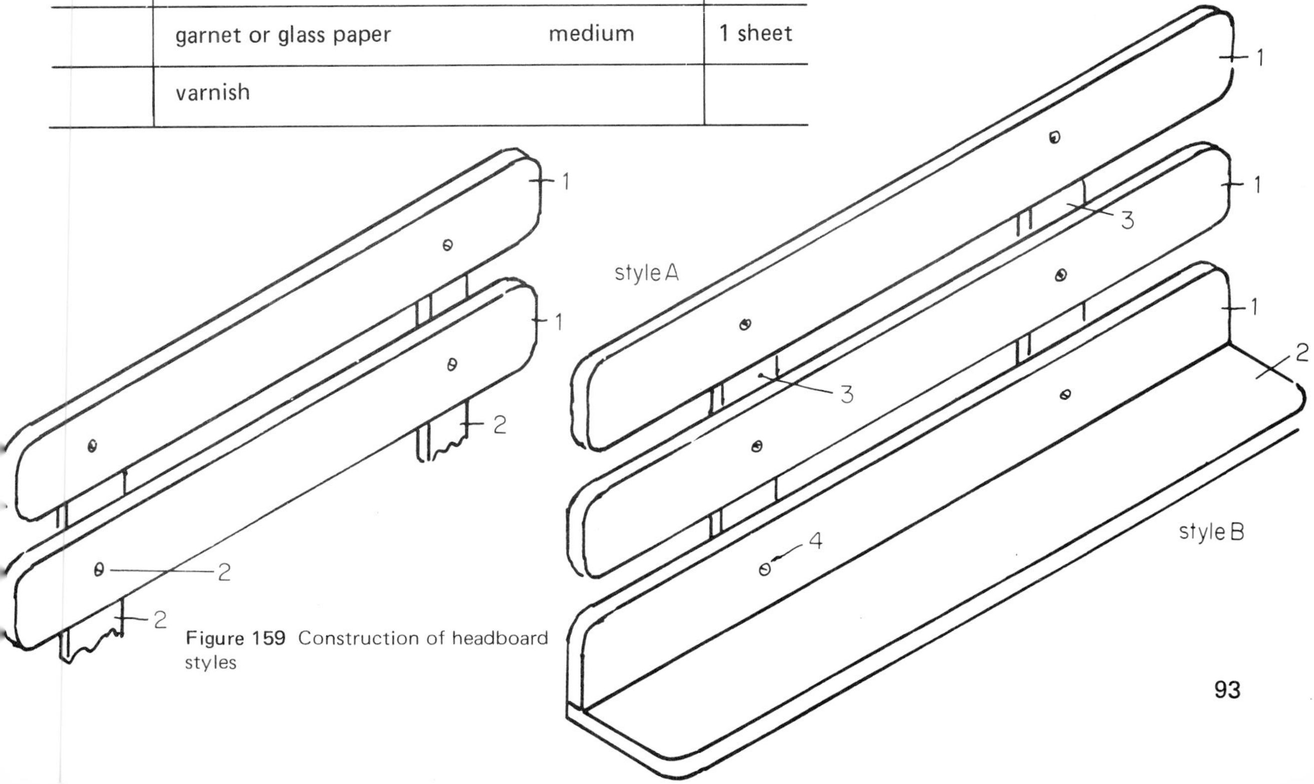

Figure 159 Construction of headboard styles

Style A — Method

1 You will see in Figure 159 that the edges of the wooden slats are rounded. This is, of course, optional. They may be left square, slightly rounded, given a totally rounded end, or chamfered.

Rounding. Mark the curve with a round object of the desired diameter, e.g. an egg-cup, tea cup, or paint tin, as shown in Figure 160.

As much as possible of the curve should be removed with one straight saw cut (Figure 160). Use your bench hook if you have one (see Tools, page 11). The timber is then Surformed to the actual curve.

2 The human eye is not the best instrument in the world for gauging the exact dimensions of any object, but it is very good indeed at telling if angles are slightly out, or if two objects are not of exactly equal size. Small differences in chamfer size will be noticed so make a template on stiff card, as shown in Figure 161, in order that all of the chamfers will be of equal size.

3 Mark the positions of the uprights (item 2) on the cross spars (item 1).

Lay the cross spars out together on a flat surface and on one of the spars measure in 150 mm (6 in) from either end.

Mark a line across both boards in these positions at 90° to the edge as shown in Figure 162. Use your square to check the accuracy of the right angles.

Using these lines as the outside edge of the uprights, lay the uprights against them and mark their positions on the slats.

4 On both boards, mark diagonals on the positions of the uprights (Figure 163) and drill through on to waste wood using a diameter of 4.5 mm ($\frac{3}{16}$ in) at the crossing points.

5 I suggest that the top of the uprights, although they are not obvious to the eye, should not be left square.

Figure 164 shows how they may be rounded or chamfered, using a Surform.

Chamfering is perhaps the most difficult if you are aiming for clean sharp edges, but if you want to try, go ahead. You can always round it off if the final effect is a bit uneven.

6 The upright does not come right to the upper edge of the top slat (see Figure 165).

Use the width of one of the uprights as a guide to draw a line about 20 mm (1 in nom) from the edge in both upright positions.

Drive two 37 mm ($1\frac{1}{2}$ in) oval brads into the upright until the points just stick through, and position the upright on the cross slat.

Check the 90° angle (shown in Figure 165) with your square and hammer the nails home.

Repeat for the other upright and reverse the assembly (Figure 165). Use brass 30 mm ($1\frac{1}{4}$ in) No. 10 countersunk screws (for appearance) and cup washers.

Rub a little ordinary soap on the thread of the screw (a common method with brass screws — it makes them easier to insert) and drive the screws home. Do not hammer them in part of the way.

7 The lower panel is fixed without nails. Only 30 mm ($1\frac{1}{4}$ in) x No. 10 brass screws with cup washers are used.

Mark a line on each upright, 50 mm (2 in) from the lower edge of the top slat, and apply glue as indicated in Figure 166.

Place the lower slat with its edge against this line and ensure that the

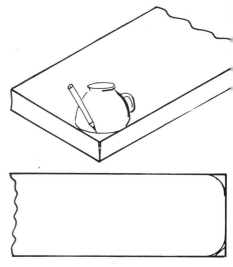

Figure 160 Shaping the ends

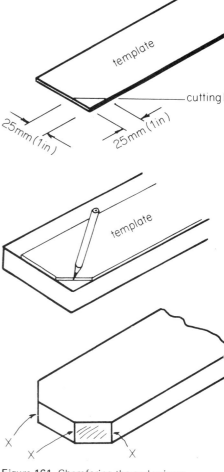

Figure 161 Chamfering the end using a template

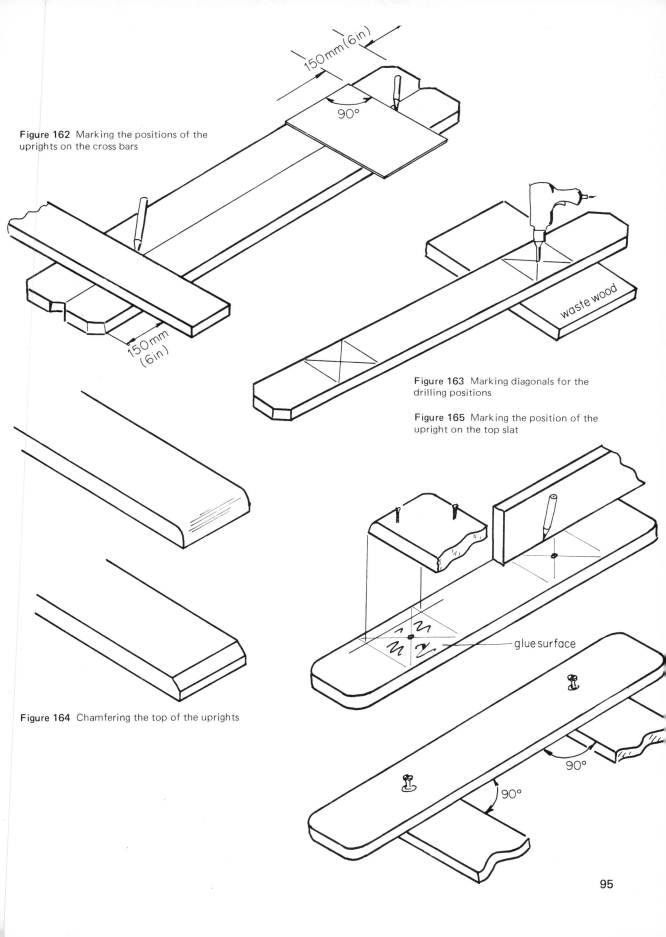

150 mm (6 in)

90°

Figure 162 Marking the positions of the
uprights on the cross bars

150 mm
(6 in)

waste wood

Figure 163 Marking diagonals for the
drilling positions

Figure 165 Marking the position of the
upright on the top slat

glue surface

90°

90°

Figure 164 Chamfering the top of the uprights

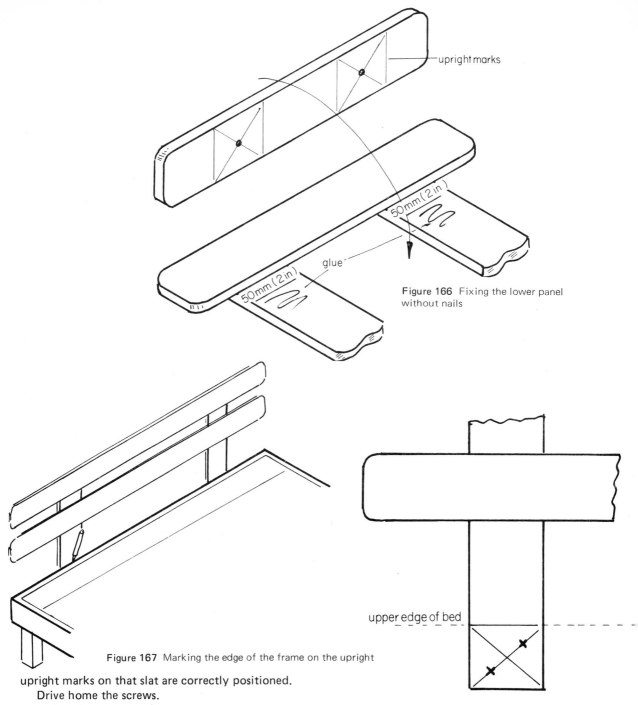

upright marks

50 mm (2 in)

50 mm (2 in)

glue

Figure 166 Fixing the lower panel without nails

Figure 167 Marking the edge of the frame on the upright

upper edge of bed

upright marks on that slat are correctly positioned.

Drive home the screws.

Wipe off excess glue.

Finish and varnish (see Finishing, page 20).

8 Position the headboard with the bottom edge of the upright against the bottom edge of the bed-frame (Figure 167).

Mark the position of the upper edge of the frame. Draw diagonals on the area of the upright which is in contact with the bed-frame (Figure 167). About a quarter of the way in from the edge of each diagonal mark the position of a 6 mm ($\frac{1}{4}$ in) fixing hole.

Fix the headboard to the bed using four 37 mm ($1\frac{1}{2}$ in) No. 10 screws through these holes.

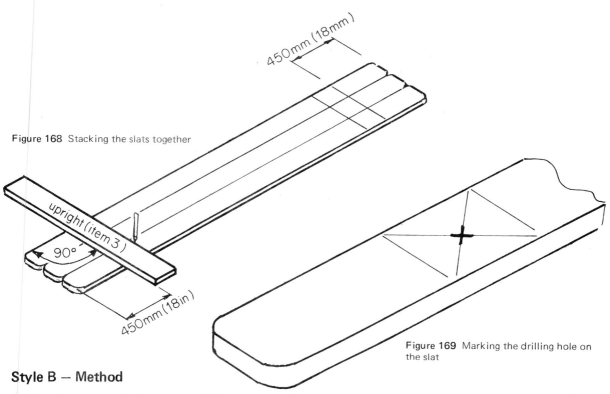

Figure 168 Stacking the slats together

Figure 169 Marking the drilling hole on the slat

Style B — Method

9 Chamfer or round the corners of the cross slats (item 1) as shown in Figures 160 and 161. Remember that the lower slat (see Figure 170) is rounded only on its two upper corners.

10 Stack the slats together (Figure 168).

Mark the position of the uprights 450 mm (18 in) in from the edge on each of the slats (item 1). Use an upright to mark the width.

Check that the upright is at 90° to the edge, using your square.

Mark diagonals on the upright positions at the end of each cross slat and drill through the diagonal crossing point (Figure 169) with a 4.5 mm ($\frac{3}{16}$ in) diameter bit.

11 The top edges of the uprights may now be rounded or chamfered as shown in Figure 164

12 Fix the top cross slat to the uprights as in Figures 163 and 165 and fix the second slat as in Figure 166.

13 Hammer three 37 mm ($1\frac{1}{2}$ in) oval brad nails into the ledge (item 2) until the tips just protrude through the plank (Figure 170). The ledge is to be nailed and glued to the cross slat so that the edges marked x in Figure 170 are flush. Hammer the three vertical nails home, and then fix with eight other nails evenly spaced along the length and fixed in dovetail fashion. The ledge/slat assembly should then be fixed to the upright with screws and glue as were the other two slats.

The headboard should now be set aside for a few hours until the glue has set. Then it should be finished and varnished (see Finishing, page 20).

The headboard is fixed to the bed with three 37 mm ($1\frac{1}{2}$ in) No. 10 screws and cup washers, i.e. two in position A and one in position B (Figure 171) drilled 6 mm ($\frac{1}{4}$ in) diameter.

The headboard ledge lies directly on the bed slats but the mattress will easily cover the small rise in level caused by the ledge.

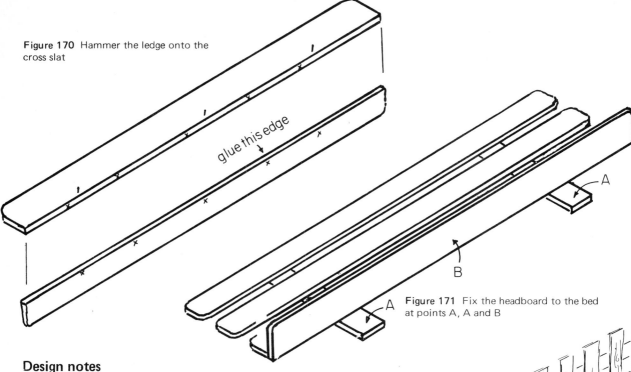

Figure 170 Hammer the ledge onto the cross slat

glue this edge

A

B

A

Figure 171 Fix the headboard to the bed at points A, A and B

Design notes

All the designers that I know of think with a pencil and paper in front of them. If you decide to try your hand at designing a headboard, then I would advise you to adopt a similar approach. It does not matter if you think that you are unable to draw, the chances are that if you cannot put your thoughts down on paper they are not yet clear enough for you to go ahead with manufacture.

It might be advisable to use a screw-and-glue assembly method in your design, rather than a nail-and-glue method. In that way you can assemble the complete structure with screws and *no* glue, then take it apart again, assured of final success when glue is used in conjunction with the screws.

Figure 172 *Above* Slats fixed vertically to two cross-spars — perhaps a capping piece of wood or an aluminium angle bar could be fitted along the top

Figure 173 *Below* Pine slats of a sheet of chipboard could be covered in a heavy texture fabric (back view)

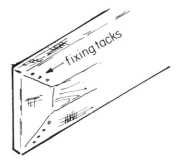

fixing tacks

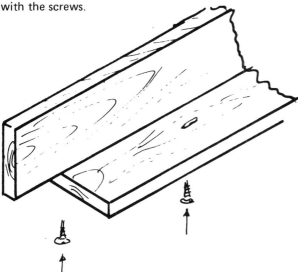

Figure 174 Extra shelving could be screwed from underneath

Points to remember

Always check 90° angles with your square.

Screws should either be countersunk into wood (see Figure 272c), dome-headed, or used with cup washers.

Check that edges which should be flush, are so in fact.

Do not be satisfied with a final finish that you feel deep down is second-best.

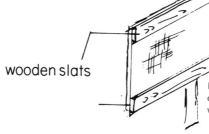

wooden slats

Figure 175 A fabric-covered headboard can be trimmed a top and bottom with wooden slats screwed to the front

Project 13
STORAGE DRAWER

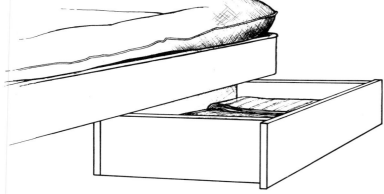

In modern houses, bedrooms are undoubtedly becoming smaller in order to give as much space as possible to the main living area. This means that no potential storage space should be wasted.

These storage drawers are designed to fit under the bed already described, but can easily be adapted to fit under any bed.

They are ideal for blanket storage, or as toy boxes in the children's room.

Materials

Item no.	Description	Quantity
1	12 mm ($\frac{1}{2}$ in) thick chipboard (particle board) 625 x 200 mm (25 x 8 in)	2
2	12 mm ($\frac{1}{2}$ in) thick chipboard 800 x 200 mm (2 ft 8 in x 8 in)	1
3	12 mm ($\frac{1}{2}$ in) thick veneered or melamine-coated chipboard (particle board) 800 x 200 mm (2 ft 8 in x 8 in)	1
4	hardboard base 590 x 725 mm ($23\frac{1}{2}$ x 29 in)	1
5	corner pads — 12 mm ($\frac{1}{2}$ in) thick chipboard (particle board) 80 x 80 mm (3 x 3 in)	4
6	pine 20 mm x 20 mm x 3 m (1 in x 1 in nom x 10 ft)	1
	PVA woodworker's adhesive	
	25 mm (1 in) oval brads	50 approx
	varnish — if wood-veneered chipboard (particle board) is used	
	garnet or glass paper medium	1 sheet

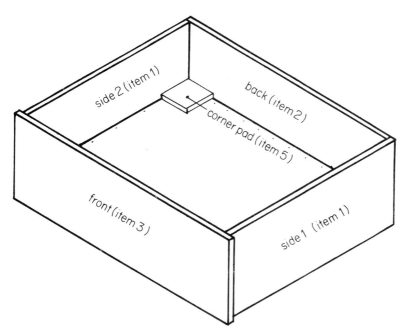

Figure 176 Construction of the storage drawer

Method

1 The back and sides are joined to the hardboard base by means of the 20 mm (1 in) square section of pine (item 6) as shown in Figure 177.

The lengths required for the back and sides are:

Back (item 2) 690 mm (27½ in)
Side 1 (item 1) 550 mm (22 in)
Side 2 (item 1) 525 mm (21 in)

It would be sensible to mark these lengths as back, side 1, and side 2 immediately after cutting them to avoid later confusion.

The lengths of beading are fixed to the back and sides with glue and 25 mm (1 in) oval brad nails as shown in Figure 178.

First apply glue.

Then position the beading 25 mm (1 in) from the end making sure that the edges marked *xxx* in the figure are flush.

Hammer home the nails — about four to each length — as indicated in Figure 178.

Punch the nails below the surface (see Nailing, page 14).

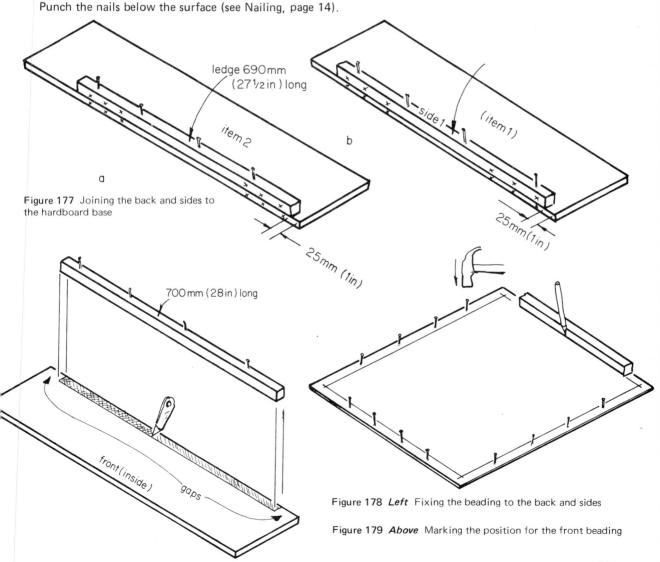

ledge 690 mm (27½ in) long

item 2

side 1 (item 1)

a

b

25 mm (1 in)

25 mm (1 in)

Figure 177 Joining the back and sides to the hardboard base

700 mm (28 in) long

front (inside) gaps

Figure 178 *Left* Fixing the beading to the back and sides

Figure 179 *Above* Marking the position for the front beading

101

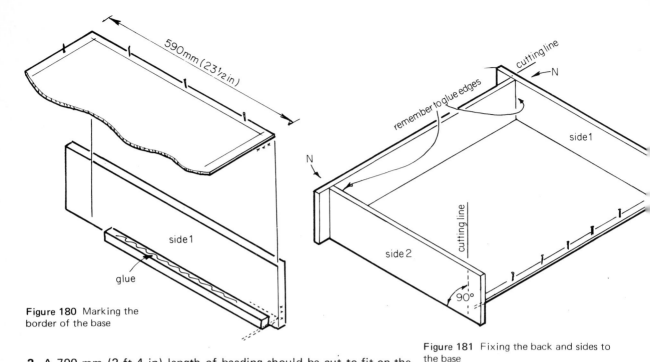

Figure 180 Marking the border of the base

Figure 181 Fixing the back and sides to the base

2 A 700 mm (2 ft 4 in) length of beading should be cut to fit on the front (item 3). It should be positioned so that the gaps at either end are equal. Mark this position (see Figure 179).

If a plastic-coated chipboard (particle board) is used, the surface must be keyed (see Figure 57, Shelving Unit).

Apply glue to this surface.

The 20 mm (1 in) square section beading can now be nailed in position using about four 25 mm (1 in) oval brads punched below the surface.

Make sure that the beading is flush with the lower edge of the front.

3 The base is to be fixed to the 20 mm (1 in nom) square section beading with nails and glue.

Hardboard is really quite a difficult material to fix nails into. To make life easier, the hardboard base (item 4) should be pre-nailed using 25 mm (1 in) oval brads.

Working on the smooth side of the hardboard and using a piece of beading as a guide, mark a strip 20 mm (1 in nom) around the border of the base as shown in Figure 180.

In the centre of this strip evenly space and hammer in four nails along each edge until their points just protrude through the other side of the board.

4 Apply glue to the ledge on side 1 (Figure 180) and position the shorter edge of the base on the ledge. Push the base firmly against the side and make sure that the edges marked *xxx* in the figure are flush with each other.

Hammer the nails home into the ledge.

Note: the side is longer than the base. This will be dealt with later.

5 The back and then side 2 are fixed in a similar manner: apply glue; hold in position; and then hammer home the nails. (Do not punch them below the surface.)

Remember to glue the vertical edges, which can be held by single nails, positioned in the direction indicated by arrows N in Figure 181.

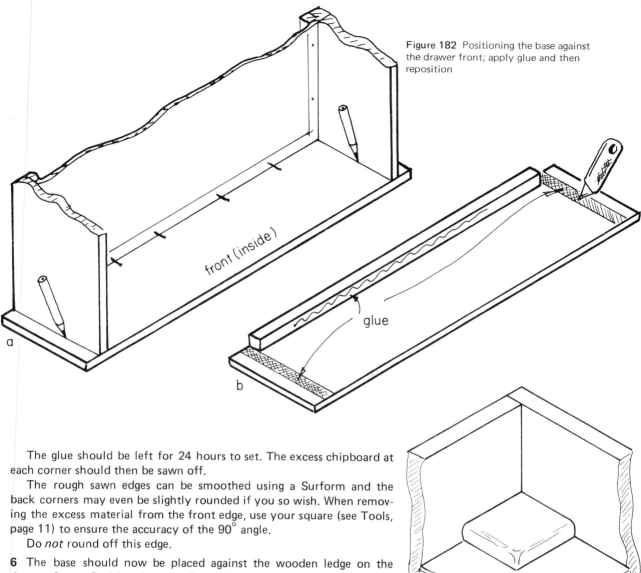

front (inside)

glue

a

b

The glue should be left for 24 hours to set. The excess chipboard at each corner should then be sawn off.

The rough sawn edges can be smoothed using a Surform and the back corners may even be slightly rounded if you so wish. When removing the excess material from the front edge, use your square (see Tools, page 11) to ensure the accuracy of the 90° angle.

Do *not* round off this edge.

6 The base should now be placed against the wooden ledge on the drawer front. Position it centrally, and mark its profile in pencil as shown in Figure 182a.

The areas where the sides and the front are in contact should be keyed if the chipboard (particle board) has a plastic coating. This is not necessary if the board has a natural wood veneer.

Figure 183 The corner pads

Apply glue as indicated in Figure 182b.

Reposition the base and hammer home the remaining nails.

Leave the drawer on its end for 24 hours while the glue between the sides and the front sets.

Lay a weighty object on top of the drawer if you can see that this is necessary to give a good tight joint.

7 Round off two of the upper edges of the chipboard (particle board) corner pads (see Figure 183) and using a liberal helping of glue, fit them into the corners using rubbed joints (see Glues and gluing, page 19). Leave glue to set.

Ball type castors as shown in Figure 184 can be fitted on to the base, on the corner pads. Fitting instructions will be provided with the castors.

The castor shown in Figure is 30 mm ($1\frac{1}{4}$ in) high. If yours are not high enough, i.e. they are less than 25 mm (1 in), you may have to put packing pieces of hardboard under them, to lift the drawer bottom clear of thick carpet pile.

Varnish finish the drawer interior and the front, if natural wood-veneered chipboard is used.

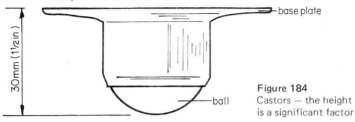

30mm (1½ in)

base plate

ball

Figure 184
Castors — the height
is a significant factor

Project 14
CHEST OF DRAWERS

The manufacture of drawers was always considered to be the job of an expert. In fact, collectors of antiques often study the dovetail joints which traditionally hold a drawer together as a guide to the quality of the article.

The drawers shown here, however, rely more on the quality of modern PVA glue than on the ability of the maker to sculpt from solid timber, working to fine degrees of accuracy.

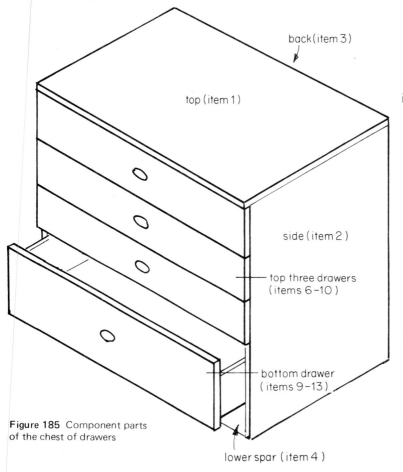

Figure 185 Component parts of the chest of drawers

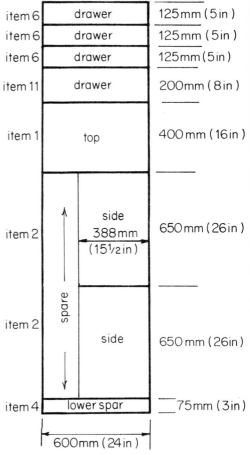

Figure 186 Cutting layout on faced chipboard (particle board) sheet, total size 2.4 m (96 in) x 600 mm (24 in)

Materials

Item no.	Description	Quantity
1	see Figure 186	1
2	see Figure 186	2
3	hardboard sheet 625 x 570 mm (25 x $22\frac{3}{4}$ in)	1
4	see Figure 186	
5	hardwood beading 25 mm (1 in) square section	6 m (20 ft)
6	see Figure 186	3
7	12 mm chipboard (particle board) 90 x 600 mm ($3\frac{1}{2}$ in x 2 ft)	3

Item no.	Description	Quantity
8	12 mm chipboard (particle board) 90 x 400 mm ($3\frac{1}{2}$ x 16 in)	6
9	hardboard 340 x 570 mm ($13\frac{1}{2}$ x $22\frac{3}{4}$ in)	4
10	25 mm (1 in) $\frac{1}{4}$-round hardwood beading	$3\frac{1}{2}$ m (12 ft)
11	see Figure 186	1
12	12 mm thick chipboard (particle board) ($\frac{1}{2}$ in) 165 x 400 mm ($5\frac{1}{2}$ x 16 in)	2
13	12 mm ($\frac{1}{2}$ in) thick chipboard (particle board) 165 x 600 mm ($5\frac{1}{2}$ in x 2 ft)	1
	PVA woodworker's adhesive	
	25 mm (1 in) oval brad nails	50 approx
	37 mm ($1\frac{1}{2}$ in) No. 8 countersunk screws and cup washers	16
	iron-on edging tape	4 m (14 ft)
	varnish — if veneered chipboard is being used	
	drawer handles	4

Method

1 To increase the glued surface between the top, sides, back, and lower spars of the chest, 25 mm (1 in) square section beading is used. An increase in glued area leads to an increase in strength, this being the principle of a joint in timber.

Cut two 300 mm (12 in) lengths of 25 mm (1 in) square beading.

By resting the side against the outside edge of the top, marking its position in pencil (see Figure 187), and subsequently laying the 25 mm (1 in) square beading against this line and marking the profile of the beading, the total glued area on the top can be seen. The beading should be placed roughly along the centre of the line.

2 If you have chosen a plastic-covered chipboard (particle board) and not a natural wood veneer — the chest of drawers illustrated is in white melamine-coated chipboard — you will have a problem with the lack of adhesion between the glue and the plastic.

To solve this, the surface being glued must be thoroughly scratched all over for at least the depth of the plastic (see Figure 188). Natural wood veneer requires no such preparation.

Next, hammer three 35 mm ($1\frac{1}{2}$ in) oval brads into the beading until their points just pierce the other side of the timber.

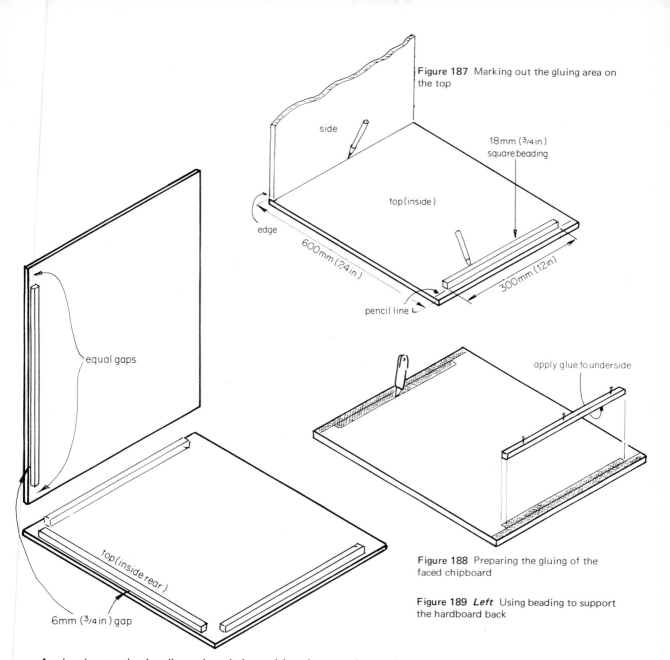

Figure 187 Marking out the gluing area on the top

side

18mm (³⁄₄ in)
square beading

top (inside)

edge

600mm (24 in)

300mm (12 in)

pencil line

equal gaps

apply glue to underside

Figure 188 Preparing the gluing of the faced chipboard

Figure 189 *Left* Using beading to support the hardboard back

top (inside rear)

6mm (³⁄₄ in) gap

Apply glue to the beading, place it in position, hammer home the nails, and punch them below the surface. (See Nailing, page 14).

Repeat this process for the next piece of beading and remember to handle gently for about two hours until the glue is set.

3 A sheet of hardboard (item 3) serves as the back of the chest. This is a most important structural component since, without it, the box would squee-gee very easily indeed. Lengths of 25 mm (1 in) square beading are glued to the top and to both sides, to support this sheet of board (see Figure 189).

The lengths of beading required are as follows: top — 1 piece 500 mm (1 ft 8 in) long; each side — 1 piece 600 mm (2 ft) long.

The beading is positioned 6 mm ($\frac{1}{4}$ in) from the back edge, with equal gaps at either end, and this should be marked on the hardboard.

If a plastic-coated board is being used, the surface must be keyed by

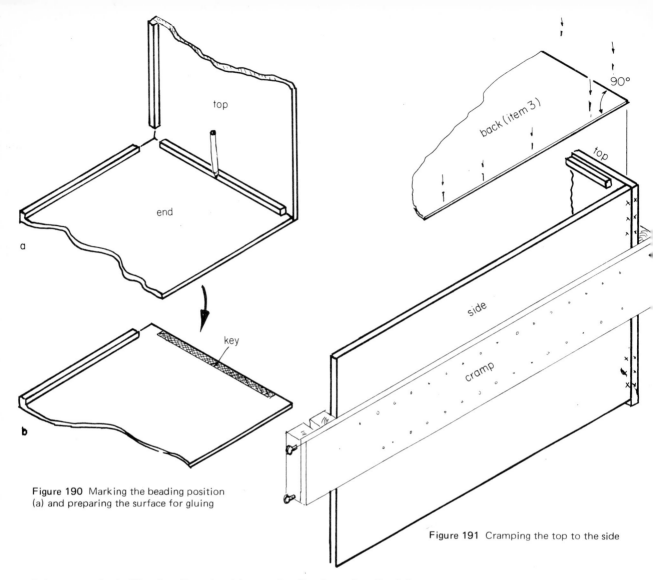

Figure 190 Marking the beading position
(a) and preparing the surface for gluing

Figure 191 Cramping the top to the side

being scratched. The beading should now be fixed as described in operation 2, Figure 188 to both ends and to the top.

4 Mark the beading position with the top and end as shown in Figure 190a and key the surface as in Figure 190b. Remember to key both sides. It is not necessary to do this for natural wood veneer.

5 Whether you are using your own adjustable cramp or a commercial one, fix the position of the adjustable bar until the side and the thickness of the top just fit (see Tools, page 13).

Apply glue to the edges which will be in contact and cramp firmly, ensuring flush edges at positions marked *xxx* (see Figure 191).

The back (item 3) should be fixed as this will ensure a 90° angle between the top and side.

Apply glue to the beading on which the back rests and then place the back in position and push firmly into the corner.

Hold it in position with 25 mm (1 in) oval brads fixed through the beading along the side and top.

Leave for 24 hours until the glue has set thoroughly.

6 When the glue used in the previous operation has set (do not try to rush it), the other side can be fixed.

108

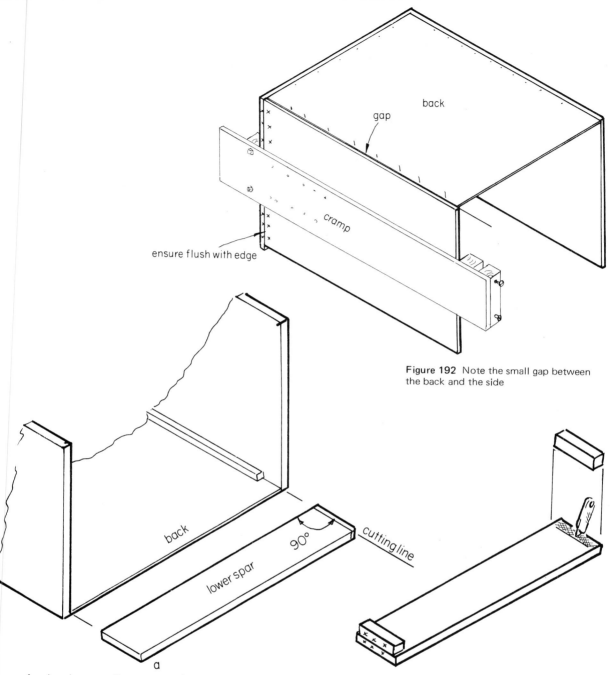

gap

back

cramp

ensure flush with edge

Figure 192 Note the small gap between the back and the side

back

lower spar

90°

cutting line

a

Figure 193 Cutting the lower spar to fit, and gluing two lengths of beading in position. Remember to key the surface of the spar if it is plastic-coated.

Apply glue to all contact edges — along the top edge and on the beading which is in contact with the back.

Fix the cramp as in Figure 192.

There will be a small gap between the back and the side as shown in Figure 192. Make sure that this gap is the same width from top to bottom before fixing into position with 25 mm (1 in) oval brads.

Allow 24 hours for the glue to set.

7 The final fitting of the lower spar will make the chest rigid. The spar will be a little long and should be sawn, then surformed if necessary until it fits neatly into the gap indicated in Figure 193.

Use your square to make sure that the angle marked 90° is accurate.

Once this part is complete, glue two lengths of 25 mm (1 in) square

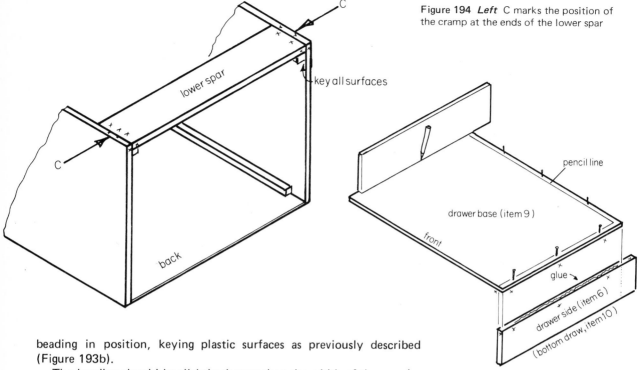

Figure 194 *Left* C marks the position of the cramp at the ends of the lower spar

Figure 195 Constructing the drawers

beading in position, keying plastic surfaces as previously described (Figure 193b).

The beading should be slightly shorter than the width of the spar (as indicated in Figure 193a) and should be fixed by the rubbed joint method. (See Glues and gluing, page 19.)

8 The contacting surfaces on the inside of the sides should be keyed if they are plastic-coated. Apply glue.

Cramp in position as indicated by arrows *C* in Figure 194.

Make sure that edges marked *xxx* in the figure are flush.

Leave for 24 hours for the glue to set.

9 Now you are ready to tackle making the drawers (Figure 195). The bottom drawer in this design is deeper than the others. This useful feature is worth the added difficulty of construction.

Round the sides and back of each hardboard drawer base mark a line the same width as the chipboard sides. Hammer in three 25 mm (1 in) oval brads along the centre of this strip on each side and the back until you can feel the nail tips coming through the chipboard.

Get a helper to hold the drawer side vertical and apply glue to the top edge. Position the base on top of this (flush at positions *x* — indicated in Figure 195) and hammer the three brads home.

The drawer side will stick out at the back a little; leave this for the moment.

10 The back of the drawer should be fitted in a similar manner.

Apply glue to the edge which butts against the side as well as to the edge which butts against the base.

Turn the drawer the right way up before fixing the nails into the corner.

Repeat this operation for the second side. Leave to dry for between three and four hours and then saw off excess material at the positions labelled cutting line in Figure 196. Take special care with the line marked with a 90° angle.

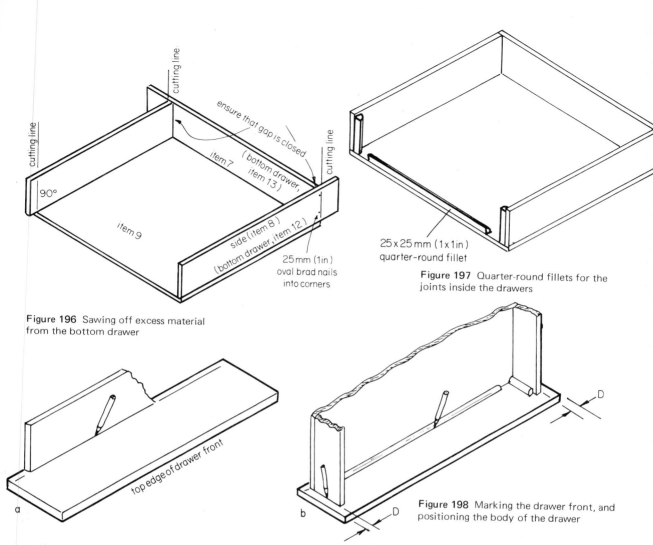

Figure 196 Sawing off excess material from the bottom drawer

Figure 197 Quarter-round fillets for the joints inside the drawers

Figure 198 Marking the drawer front, and positioning the body of the drawer

Use your square to check this angle.

Finish the sawn edges with a Surform if necessary.

11 Cut lengths of 25 mm x 25 mm (1 in x 1 in) $\frac{1}{4}$-round fillet to sizes that will fit the drawers approximately (as indicated in Figure 197).

Apply glue to the fillets and hold them in position by the rubbed joint method. If the joints do not look tight, a heavy object laid in the centre of the longer length of fillet should do the trick. Ensure that the edges are flush.

12 Mark each drawer front with a pencil line the thickness of a piece of 12 mm ($\frac{1}{2}$ in) chipboard away from the bottom edge as shown in Figure 198a.

Position the drawer body with its lower edge on the pencil line.

Make sure that the gaps marked D in Figure 198b are exactly equal. Pencil right round the edges as indicated in Figure 198b to mark the area that is to be glued.

Plastic-covered chipboard must be keyed over this area.

Apply glue to this area.

Reposition the drawer body and hold it in place with a heavy weight such as a brick or two.

Leave for a few hours for the glue to set.

111

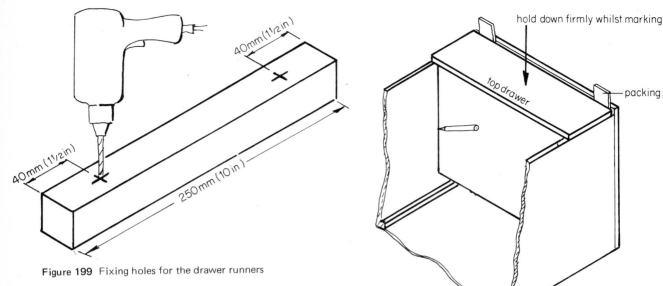

Figure 199 Fixing holes for the drawer runners

Figure 200 Marking the positions for the drawer runners

13 Drawer runners are made from the same 25 mm (1 in) square section hardwood that was used in the framing.

For four drawers there are eight runners, each 250 mm (10 in) long.

Cut these to length and mark the positions of the two fixing holes as shown in Figure 199. Drill through each of these two positions with a 4.5 mm ($\frac{3}{16}$ in) diameter drill.

The positions shown are approximate; since drawer runners are never seen, accuracy is not required.

Repeat this operation for all six runners.

14 The drawers are spaced during the fixing of the runners by the use of two packing pieces each about 3-4 mm ($\frac{1}{8}$ in-$\frac{3}{16}$ in) thick. These can be scraps of hardboard or plywood.

Lay the chest on its back and place the top drawer in position as in Figure 200.

Hold the drawer down firmly and at the same time push it against the packing pieces to keep a uniform gap between the drawer and the top surface.

Now mark the bottom edges of the drawers on both sides as indicated in Figure 200.

15 If you are using plastic-coated chipboard, the area to which the runner is to be fixed should be keyed.

First mark the profile of the runner about 40 mm ($1\frac{1}{2}$ in) from the front of the chest, with its upper edge along the line drawn in operation 14 as shown in Figure 201a.

After keying accurately re-position the runner. Hold it firmly in position and, in order to make the screwing easier, hammer two nails into the chipboard for about 6 mm ($\frac{1}{4}$ in) through the runner fixing holes (Figure 201b).

Remove the nails.

Apply glue to the underside of the runner and screw it in position using 37 mm ($1\frac{1}{2}$ in) No. 8 screws with cup washers.

Repeat the process for the other runner.

With the chest the right way up, try the drawer in position.

If you have made a bad error which involves moving one of the runners, remove the screws and move the runner about 10 mm ($\frac{1}{2}$ in)

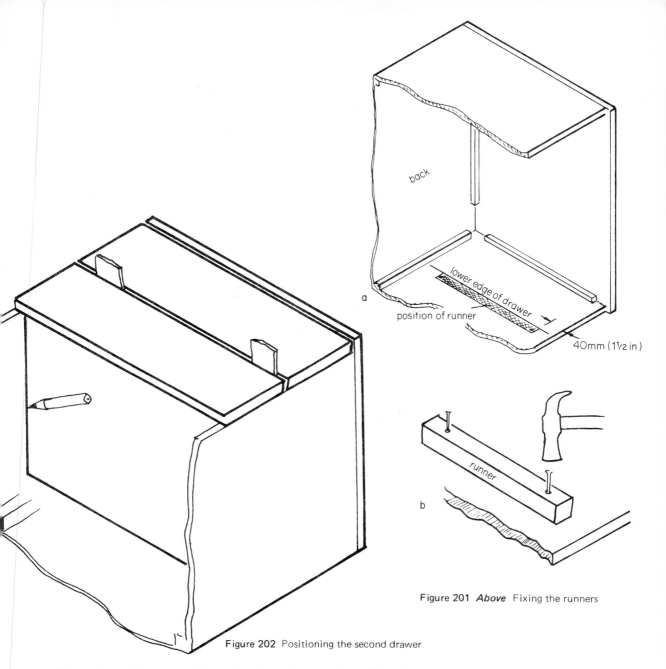

back

a

lower edge of drawer

position of runner

40mm (1½ in)

runner

b

Figure 201 *Above* Fixing the runners

Figure 202 Positioning the second drawer

out of the old position to avoid screwing into the wrongly-positioned holes.

16 The second drawer is positioned in very much the same way as the first (Figure 202).

The first drawer should be positioned and held firmly against the runners. Position the packing pieces as shown in Figue 200. Place the drawer runners as shown in Figure 201.

Repeat until all the drawer runners are fixed.

Add iron-on tape edges (see Finishing, page 20) but do not bother about lower edges of drawer fronts. Finish by varnishing if veneered chipboard has been used.

To enable the drawers to run freely, rub an ordinary candle once or twice along each runner.

113

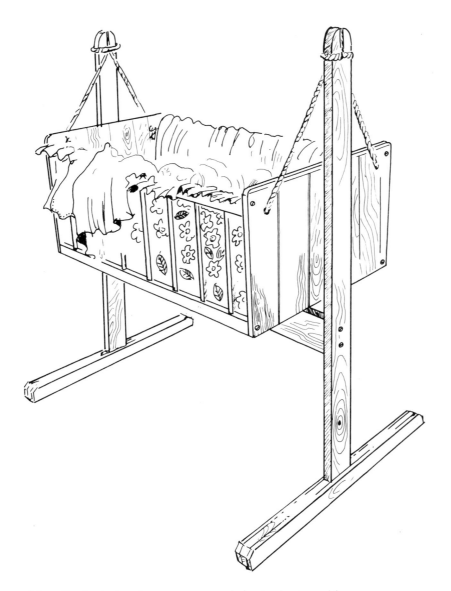

Logically speaking, the best place for a very young baby to sleep would be in a solid wooden box, lined with a thick warm blanket. Logic, however, has nothing to do with welcoming a baby into the house, and why on earth should it have?

Our own baby slept in a cradle exactly the same as the one described here, for about the first six months — until she began to show some signs of sitting up. Both young Angela and the cradle were the subjects of numerous pleasing compliments.

In fact at the time of writing the cradle is on the point of being re-assembled for baby number two. It *is* re-usable!

The cradle can be quickly taken to pieces for storage.

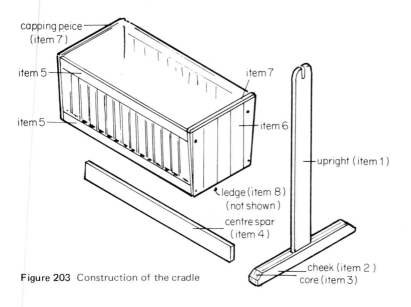

Figure 203 Construction of the cradle

Materials

Item no.	Description	Quantity
1	dressed pine 95 mm x 20 mm x 1.2 m (4 in x 1 in nom x 4 ft)	2
2	dressed pine 45 x 12 x 600 mm (2 in x $\frac{1}{2}$ in nom x 2 ft)	4
3	dressed pine 45 x 20 x 300 mm (2 in x 1 in nom x 1 ft)	4
4	dressed pine 95 x 20 x 900 mm (4 in x 1 in nom x 3 ft)	1
5	dressed pine 45 x 20 x 830 mm (2 in x 1 in nom x 2 ft 9 in)	4
6	red pine tongued-and-grooved lining 400 mm (16 in) long	10
7	hardwood beading 12 mm ($\frac{1}{2}$ in) square section 500 mm (1 ft 8 in) long	2
8	dressed pine 20 x 20 x 400 mm (1 in x 1 in nom x 1 ft 4 in)	2
9*	9.5 mm ($\frac{3}{8}$ in) diameter hardwood dowel 375 mm (15 in) long	22

Item no.	Description		Quantity
	37 mm (1½ in) No. 8 wood screws with cup washers		12
	25 mm (1 in) oval brad nails		50 approx
	plastic masonry plugs suitable for screw sizes 6, 8, and 10 — actual outside diameter of plug is 6 mm (¼ in)		12
	varnish to finish		
	PAV woodworker's adhesive		
	garnet or glass paper	medium fine	1 sheet 1 sheet
	cradle lining: 135 cm wide 100 cm long (54 in wide 1¼ yd long)		
	Velcro fastening 2 cm wide 250 cm long (¾ in wide 10 in long)		

*If your drill chuck will not expand to take a 9.5 mm (⅜ in) bit, you should use a dowel of a diameter equal to the largest bit you can use.

The cradle is supported on natural hemp rope which slips into a slot in the upright. This slot is quite difficult to make but remember that slight imperfections will be hidden to a great extent by the rope so you should not worry too much.

Method

The method described in operations 1 and 2 gives success if care is taken.

1 First mark the position of the slot as follows: take a strip of paper the same width as the upright (Figure 204a) and fold it along its centre. Mark two pin-pricks through the paper, each 6 mm (¼ in) from the fold (Figure 204b). Open the paper out — there are *four* pin-pricks in it — and place it over the upright. Mark through each of the pin-pricks into wood (Figure 204c).

2 Join up the pin-pricks with two lines. This indicates the marking for a centrally-positioned 12 mm (½ in) slot.

Now comes the tricky bit. Drill two 6 mm (¼ in) diameter holes about 70 mm (3 in) from the top edge so that the edge of each hole just touches the slot markings (Figure 205a).

Now saw out the slot keeping the saw kerf (or slot) just to the inside of the line (Figure 205b).

The inside edges of the slot can be tidied up with medium grade garnet or glass paper wrapped round a slim flat object, such as a ruler or tea knife, and the end can be tackled with the same grade of abrasive wrapped round a pencil.

Repeat the procedure for the other upright.

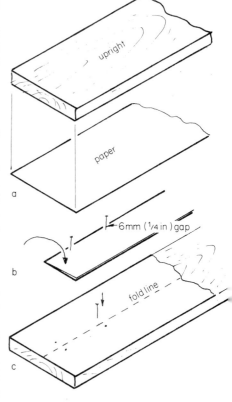

Figure 204 Marking the position of the slot in the upright

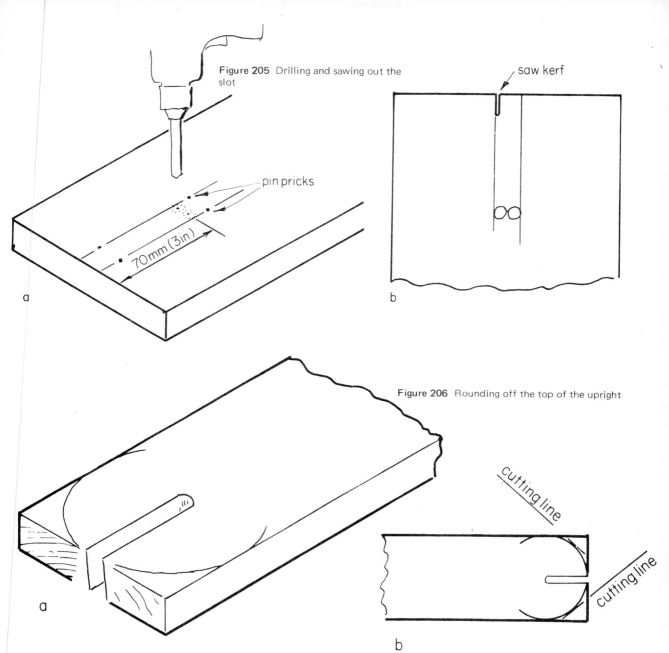

Figure 205 Drilling and sawing out the slot

pin pricks

70mm (3in)

a

saw kerf

b

Figure 206 Rounding off the top of the upright

cutting line

cutting line

a

b

3 The top of the upright can now be rounded off.

Find a round container (a paint pot, perhaps) which is about the same distance across as the upright. Mark the top of the upright as close to a semi-circle as possible, using the container as a guide (Figure 206a).

With a single saw cut per corner, remove as much material as possible and surform (see surforming, page 20) down to the semi-circle (Figure 206b).

4 The centre spar will be fixed to the upright with two screws and the positions of these screws must now be found.

Holding the two uprights together on a flat surface (Figure 207a) lay the centre spar across both of them with its lower edge 300 mm (12 in) from the bottom.

Check the 90° angle shown in the figure with your square (see Tools, page 11).

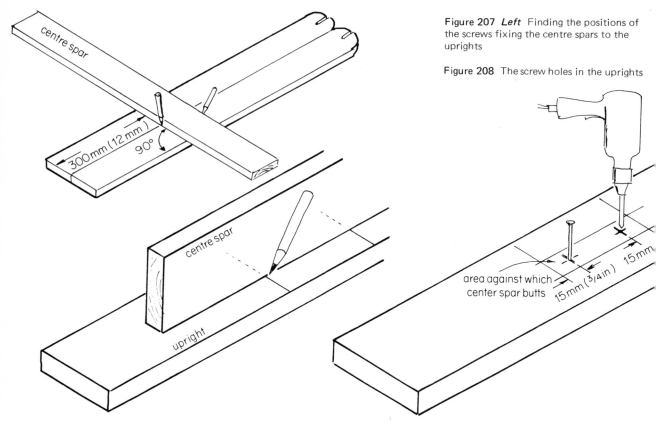

Mark across the uprights on either side of this centre spar.

Next lay the centre spar *centrally* as shown in Figure 207b (check that it is centred with a tape measure) and mark its position. (See Figure 208 if further clarification is required.)

5 The screw holes should be marked as shown in Figure 208 15 mm ($\frac{3}{4}$ in) from the top and bottom of the central spar, and as close to the centre of the marked rectangle as you can get it judging by eye.

In each of these positions, hammer a nail in for about 6 mm ($\frac{1}{4}$ in) to give the drill a lead, then drill through, with a 5 mm ($\frac{3}{16}$ in) diameter bit.

6 Two holes must be drilled into the centre spar end grain in exactly the same relative positions as the two holes described in the previous operation.

First, as shown in Figure 209a, hammer two 25 mm (1 in) oval brads about half-way in on the line.

Now with a helper holding the centre spar down firmly on a work surface, and resting the two temporary nails on the spar, as shown in Figure 209b, place the upright in the correct position. Drill through the two holes in the upright using a 5 mm ($\frac{3}{16}$ in) diameter drill bit until the drill has entered the end grain of the centre spar by roughly 5 mm ($\frac{3}{16}$ in).

Now mark the spar and the upright with corresponding identification marks, to ensure that they are always assembled in this way. The marks X should always line up before assembly as shown in Figure 209b.

Remove the upright.

7 Change over to a 6 mm ($\frac{1}{4}$ in) drill bit and drill into the spar on its own, for about 50 mm (2 in). (Wrap a piece of tape round the drill bit to act as a depth gauge.)

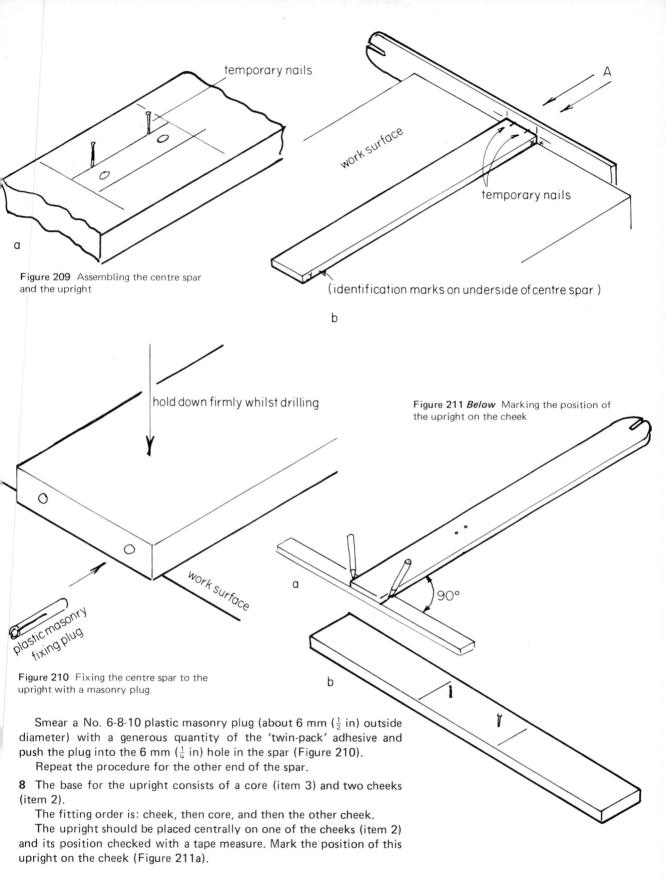

temporary nails

work surface

A

temporary nails

(identification marks on underside of centre spar)

a

Figure 209 Assembling the centre spar
and the upright

b

hold down firmly whilst drilling

Figure 211 *Below* Marking the position of
the upright on the cheek

work surface

plastic masonry
fixing plug

a

90°

Figure 210 Fixing the centre spar to the
upright with a masonry plug

b

Smear a No. 6-8-10 plastic masonry plug (about 6 mm ($\frac{1}{2}$ in) outside
diameter) with a generous quantity of the 'twin-pack' adhesive and
push the plug into the 6 mm ($\frac{1}{4}$ in) hole in the spar (Figure 210).

Repeat the procedure for the other end of the spar.

8 The base for the upright consists of a core (item 3) and two cheeks
(item 2).

The fitting order is: cheek, then core, and then the other cheek.

The upright should be placed centrally on one of the cheeks (item 2)
and its position checked with a tape measure. Mark the position of this
upright on the cheek (Figure 211a).

119

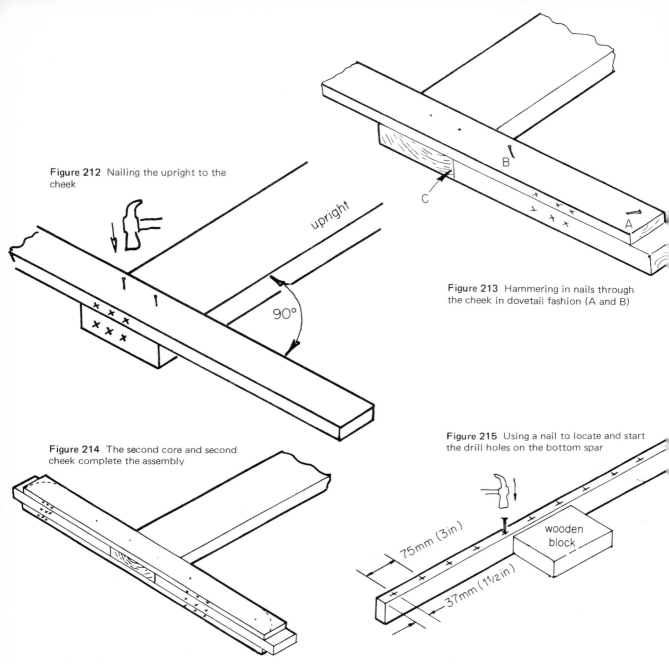

Figure 212 Nailing the upright to the cheek

upright

90°

Figure 213 Hammering in nails through the cheek in dovetail fashion (A and B)

Figure 214 The second core and second cheek complete the assembly

Figure 215 Using a nail to locate and start the drill holes on the bottom spar

75mm (3 in)

37mm (1½ in)

wooden block

Two 25 mm (1 in) oval brads are then hammered into this area on the cheek until the points can be felt with the finger-tips, as they come through the other side (Figure 211b).

9 Apply glue, then re-position the cheek.

Check that the edges marked *xxx* in Figure 212 are flush and that the 90° angle shown in the figure is correct. The accuracy of the angle is most important when fitting this first cheek.

Hammer the nails home, and punch below the surface (see Nailing, page 14).

Wipe off excess glue.

10 Smear one face of one of the core pieces (item 3) with glue and position it as shown in Figure 213. The core is slightly long — this is all right at this stage. Check that the edges marked *xxx* in the figure are

120

flush and that the joint is closed tightly at the point indicated by arrow C.

Hammer in two 25 mm (1 in) oval brads in dovetail fashion (see Nailing, page 14). First nail A then nail B (see Figure 213).

If the core is now fixed quite tightly, then leave it, (the fewer nails the better). But if there is an unsightly gap somewhere, fix another dovetail pair of nails.

Punch nails below the surface.

Wipe off excess glue.

11 Fix the other core, then the second cheek, until the base is as shown in Figure 214.

In all of these operations make do with as few nails as possible, but use the glue fairly liberally. Always remember, though, to wipe off any excess glue immediately the joint has been made.

The actual number of nails used must be for you to decide, but if you find that the pieces of wood are so warp-free that one nail, hammered vertically, will keep the joint tight, then use only one nail.

In a case like that, however, you would lay the job aside for between 45 minutes and $1\frac{1}{2}$ hours to allow the glue to partly set before proceeding further with assembly.

Both uprights are fixed in an identical fashion.

The end assemblies should be left for 24 hours to set before rounding off the corners using a suitable round container as a guide (see dotted lines in Figure 214), and following the procedure outlined in operation 3.

The sides consist of a top and a bottom spar (item 5) joined together by 9.5 mm ($\frac{3}{8}$ in) hardwood dowels.

12 The positions of the dowel on the bottom spar are fixed as follows.

Mark a point 37 mm ($1\frac{1}{2}$ in) from the end of one of the items 5 and mark eleven other points each 75 mm (3 in) apart. This should leave a space of approximately 37 mm ($1\frac{1}{2}$ in) at the other end of the bottom spar.

At these twelve points, mark crosses as centrally as possible. This can be done without measuring if you have a good eye.

In order to give the drill a start and to reduce the risk of a misplaced hole hammer a nail 5 mm ($\frac{3}{16}$ in) into each of these positions and then remove it (Figure 215).

Drill through each of these positions with a 9.5 mm ($\frac{3}{8}$ in) diameter bit.

Both the drill and the wood must be kept as vertical as possible during this operation. The angle of the drill is up to you, but the actual spar can be held against a block of scrap wood by a helper (Figure 215). It can thus easily be held rigid in a vertical position.

13 The drilled spar should be held against another (undrilled) spar and both spars marked with a letter B as in Figure 216a to ensure that they will always be used as a pair in that relative position.

Ensure that the edges marked with Xs are flush with each other, and drill through one existing end position, and subsequently the undrilled spar, to a depth of about 10 mm ($\frac{1}{2}$ in). Push a small piece of 9.5 mm ($\frac{3}{8}$ in) diameter dowel through both spars, thus holding the two ends together (Figure 216b).

Repeat this operation for the other end of the spars.

Now with both ends fixed, drill through the other nine positions ensuring that the edges marked *xxx* are always flush.

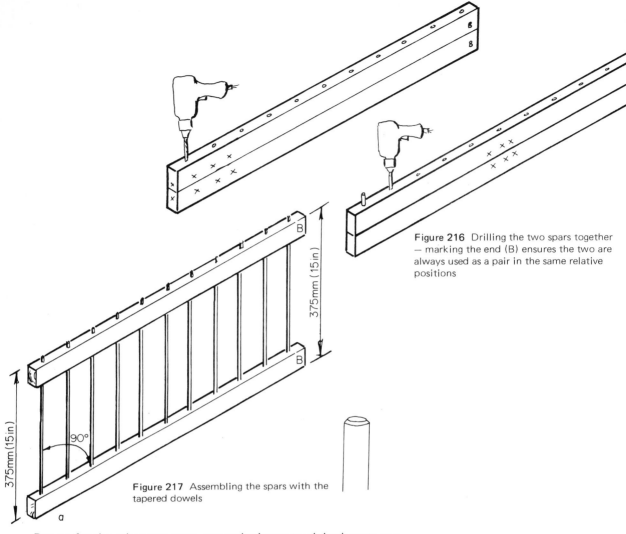

Figure 216 Drilling the two spars together — marking the end (B) ensures the two are always used as a pair in the same relative positions

Figure 217 Assembling the spars with the tapered dowels

Repeat for the other two spars, remembering to mark both spars as a pair.

14 The 10 mm ($\frac{1}{2}$ in) deep holes drilled in the spars during operation 13 should now be further drilled to at least 25 mm (1 in). Mark the distance on your drill bit with a piece of tape and drill to ensure this minimum depth.

15 Cut 22 pieces of dowel each 450 mm (18 in) long and taper the ends as shown in Figure 217b. A pencil sharpener should do this very easily.

Drop a liberal blob of glue into each blind hole in the lower spar in Figure 217a and push a dowel firmly into each hole.

Now things may get tricky so a pair of extra hands will not go amiss.

Smear the other end of each dowel with glue and complete the assembly as shown in Figure 217a. Make sure that the pairing marks, labelled B in the figure, are correctly positioned.

Check that the total height at *each* end is 375 mm (15 in) and that the 90° angle shown is not too far out.

Wipe off excess glue.

The spare pieces of dowel sticking through the spar can be trimmed off after the glue has half set, which takes about forty minutes.

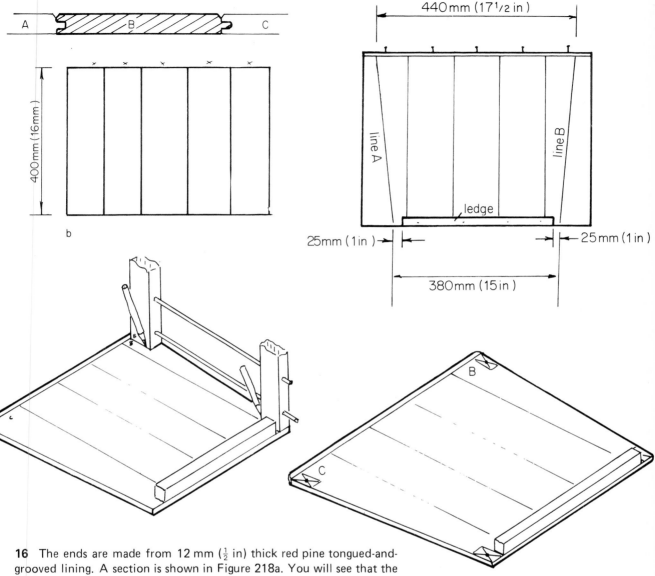

A   B   C

400 mm (16 mm)

b

440 mm (17½ in)

line A

line B

ledge

25 mm (1 in) →

← 25 mm (1 in)

380 mm (15 in)

B

C

16 The ends are made from 12 mm ($\frac{1}{2}$ in) thick red pine tongued-and-grooved lining. A section is shown in Figure 218a. You will see that the tongue of A fits into the groove of B, and so on.

The material is normally sold in lengths, which are about 100 mm (4 in) wide, not including the tongue.

Make sure that at least one edge is flush (marked with *x*s in Figure 218b) and make up a board about 500 mm (20 in) wide.

In each case, apply a smear of glue to the tongue before fitting the lengths together.

No nails should be required.

Wipe off excess glue and lay aside until the glue has set.

17 The ends should be approximately 440 mm (17$\frac{1}{2}$ in) across the top and 380 mm (15$\frac{1}{2}$ in) across the bottom. The important point is that the lines marked *A* and *B* in Figure 219 must *not* cross any of the tongue-and-groove joints.

Once these lines are marked, the capping piece (item 7) should be glued and nailed in position, as indicated, using 25 mm (1 in) oval brads punched below the surface.

Figure 218 *Top left* The ends are constructed from tongued-and-grooved lining

Figure 219 *Top right* Ensure that lines A and B do not cross any of the tongued-and-grooved joints

Figure 220 *Above left* Positioning the cradle sides on the ends

Figure 221 *Above* Locating the drilling holes

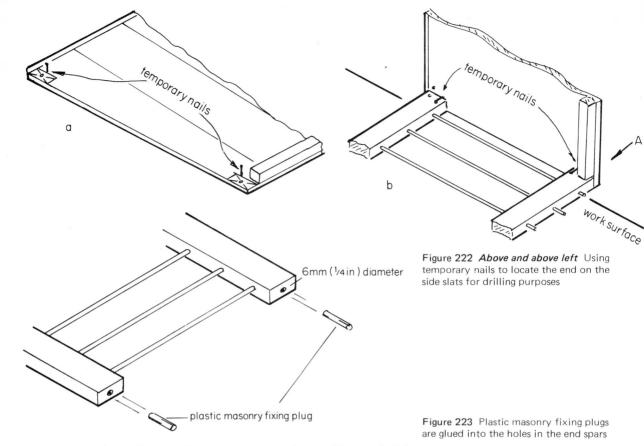

temporary nails

a

temporary nails

A

b

work surface

6mm (¼ in) diameter

plastic masonry fixing plug

Figure 222 *Above and above left* Using temporary nails to locate the end on the side slats for drilling purposes

Figure 223 Plastic masonry fixing plugs are glued into the holes in the end spars

The ledge (item 8) should now be cut to a length 25 mm (1 in) shorter than the distance across the bottom (see Figure 219). Glue and nail the ledge into position using about six 37 mm ($1\frac{1}{2}$ in) oval brad nails in dovetail fashion (see Nailing, page 14).

Wipe off excess glue and leave to set for at least three hours before sawing along lines A and B. Remove the saw marks with a Surform.

18 Position the sides over the end as shown in Figure 220.

Lightly pencil identification marks on the end, making sure that this will be the final assembled position, and mark the profile of the side slats as shown. These identification marks are important, since the ends are not likely to be exactly identical and they must therefore be assembled in a certain order each time.

Repeat the procedure for both ends.

19 Draw diagonals on each of the rectangular profiles which were marked in operation 18 (note the identification marks B and C in Figure 221). Drill through in each of the diagonal crossing positions (four per end) with a 4 mm ($\frac{3}{16}$ in) diameter drill.

20 The end should now be held against the side so that holes can be drilled through these positions into the end grain of the side slats. This will ensure that the hole spacing in the ends and the sides is identical.

Hammer two 25 mm (1 in) oval brads half-way into the profile line of the side slats as marked in the ends (Figure 222).

Hold the side firmly down on a work surface and correctly position the end with the temporary nails resting on the side slats (Figure 222b).

Using a 4 mm ($\frac{3}{16}$ in) drill bit, drill through into the end grain of the slats for about 6 mm ($\frac{1}{4}$ in) as indicated by arrow A on Figure 222b.

Repeat for the other side slat, without moving the end.

Carry out this operation for the holes at both ends of each side slat.

Do not forget to match up those identification marks!

21 Using a 6 mm ($\frac{1}{4}$ in) drill bit, marked with tape at a depth of 50 mm (2 in), drill to that depth all the existing 4 mm ($\frac{3}{16}$ in) holes in the end spars.

Smear plastic No. 6-8-10 masonry plugs (about 6 mm ($\frac{1}{4}$ in) outside diameter) with twin-pack glue and push the plugs into the holes until they are flush with the surface (Figure 223).

Leave until the glue has set thoroughly. (Check the instructions on the packet for timing.)

22 Before moving on to the final assembly, finish and varnish the various component parts (see Finishing, page 20).

The various assembly identification marks should be remade on parts which will be hidden in the completed cradle. Examples of proper final positions for assembly identification marks are shown in Figure 224.

23 The cradle should be fairly low for stability and therefore the rope length can only be determined by trial and error.

To hold the rope to the upright, simply loop it over as shown in Figure 225. Knots in natural fibre do not tend to slip, so there is no need to worry about safety.

No size was given for the base in the list of materials, since it should be a fairly close fit at the end ledges and this distance is best measured after the final assembly.

No support is required in the centre of the base, but for your own peace of mind, why not lay a set of bathroom scales in the cradle, and push down on the scales until they read about 18 kg (40 lb)? This is about twice the weight of the heaviest six-month-old baby.

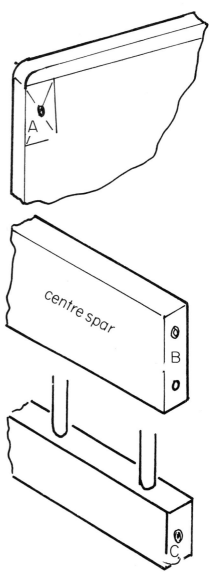

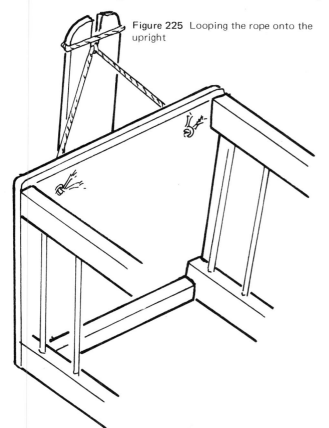

Figure 225 Looping the rope onto the upright

Figure 224 Final assembly identification marks — make them where they will be invisible in the completed cradle

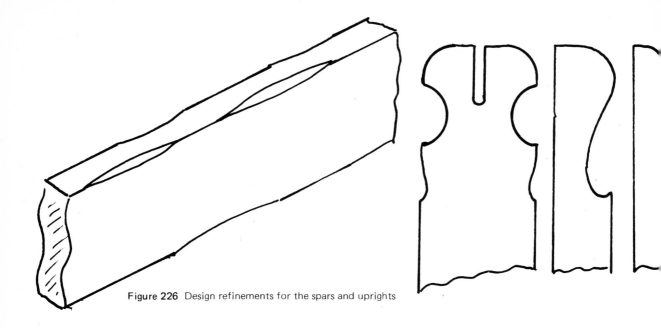

Figure 226 Design refinements for the spars and uprights

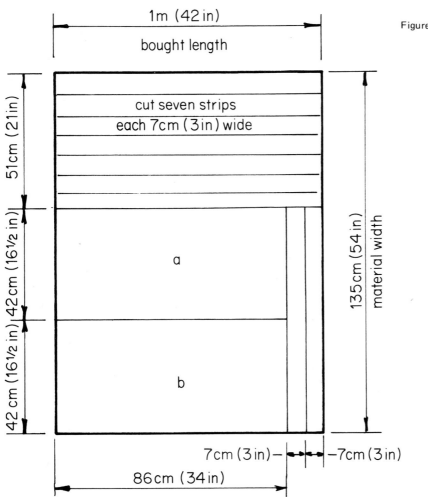

Figure 227 Cutting layout for the fabric

1m (42 in)

bought length

cut seven strips
each 7cm (3in) wide

51cm (21in)

135cm (54 in)
material width

42 cm (16½ in)

a

42 cm (16½ in)

b

7cm (3in)— —7cm (3in)

86cm (34 in)

24 You can add refinements to the cradle if you wish. An 'olde-worlde' look can be produced by paring away the edges of the uprights and spars with a sharp knife. This gives the cradle the appearance of having been finished with a spoke-shave. Do not overdo this. Give these edges a final rub down with medium grade glass paper (see Figure 226a).

The top of the uprights can be 'figured' if you can lay your hands on a power drill with a jig-saw attachment.

The best way to do this is to take a strip of paper the same width as the upright, fold it in half, mark the pattern you want to reproduce, and then cut it out.

Trace round the pattern on the upright and then cut out (see Figure 226b for suggestions).

Remember: the best designs are simple ones.

25 Cut two pieces of material (labelled *a* and *b* in Figure 227) each measuring 42 cm x 86 cm (1 ft 4½ in x 2 ft 10 in). From the remaining material cut seven strips 7 cm (3 in) wide and 1 m (1¼ yd) long, and two strips 7 cm (3 in) wide and 84 cm (2 ft 9 in) long, for the frills. Figure 227 shows the cutting layout.

Pin a 2 cm (1 in) hem right round *a* and *b*.

Tack and sew.

Join the 7 cm (3 in) wide strips together to make two strips 4.30 m (14 ft 3 in) long. These measurements do not need to be exact.

26 Hem both edges of the two strips with a 1 cm ($\frac{1}{2}$ in) hem, tucking under the raw edges. Then with a piece of thread 170 cm (5 ft 7 in) long (the length of three sides of pieces *a* or *b*) sew one of the strips up the middle with medium-length (1½-2 cm ($\frac{1}{2}$-$\frac{3}{4}$ in)) running stitches (Figure 228). Repeat for the second strip.

The material will gather. Evenly adjust the gathers, and fit the resulting frill round three edges of *a*, leaving one long side free, and placing the wrong side of the frill to the right side of rectangle *a* along the hem-line. Pin, again adjusting the gathers to fit. Tack and sew (see Figure 228). Repeat the procedure for rectangle *b*.

Sew strips of Velcro 2 cm ($\frac{3}{4}$ in) wide 5 cm (2 in) long to the wrong side of the material as shown in Figure 228.

Fix matching Velcro to the slatted sides of the cradle, in positions corresponding to those on the material. (See Figure 228.) This is easily done using an ordinary office stapling machine.

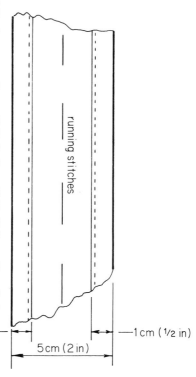

running stitches

1cm (½ in)— 5cm (2 in) —1cm (½ in)

Figure 228 *Above and left* Making the gathered frill

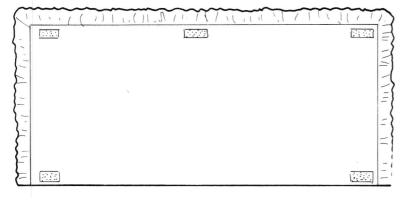

BABY-WALKER

Judging by the dogged determination with which most babies learn to walk, it must be one of the most exciting and challenging periods of life. Furniture has only one purpose to the toddler, it serves as hand-holds and staging-posts in his battle to become bi-pedal. To have a device, therefore, which enables 'junior' to go where he or she wants must make the thrill of the Wright Brothers' first airborne excursion appear mundane by comparison.

This is a sure-fire winner. You can be certain that the user will not be interested in the finer details of the surface finish — just keep it smooth and safe.

The most important principle of the baby-walker is that the handle lies *inside* the wheel base, thus ensuring stability.

Materials

Item no.	Description	Quantity
1	dressed pine 95 x 20 x 500 mm (4 in x 1 in nom x 1 ft 8 in)	2
2	dressed pine 45 x 20 x 500 mm (2 in x 1 in x 1 ft 8 in)	2
3	veneered chipboard (particle board) 75 x 300 x 12 mm (3 in x 1 ft x $\frac{1}{2}$ in)	2

Item no.	Description	Quantity
4	veneered chipboard (particle board) 440 x 300 x 12 (17½ in)	1
	N.B. Items 3 and 4 should be cut from the same 300 mm (12 in) wide board.	
5	hardwood dowel 25 mm diameter x 260 mm long (1 in diameter x 10½ in long)	1
6*	95 mm (4 in) diameter wheels	4
	9.5 mm ($\frac{1}{4}$ in) diameter axle	2
	spring hub caps	4
7	37 mm (1½ in) No. 8 countersunk screws with cup washers	2
	25 mm (1 in) oval brads	10 approx
	PVA woodworker's adhesive	
	varnish to finish	

*See suppliers, page 165.

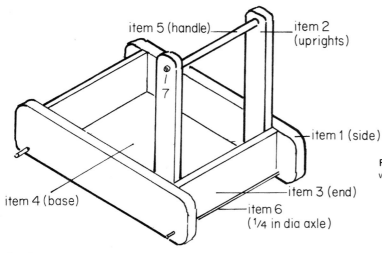

item 5 (handle)

item 2 (uprights)

item 1 (side)

item 4 (base)

item 3 (end)

item 6 (¼ in dia axle)

Figure 229 Construction of the baby walker

Method

1 First fix the axle position.

This is important not only because it is the basis of the stability of the apparatus, but also because the rubber wheels must stick out from the front of the wooden body providing a fender to protect your furniture.

Use one of the 20 mm (1 in nom) thick sides to mark the distance of the axle from the lower edge of the other side (item 1) (Figure 230).

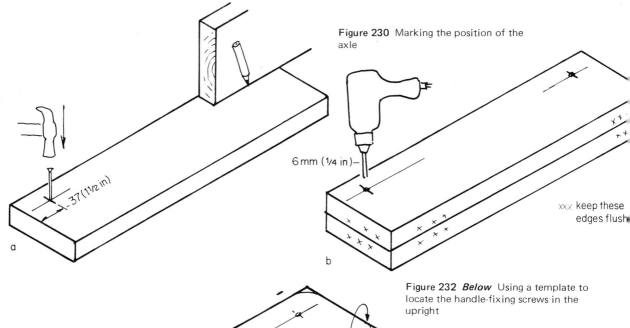

Figure 230 Marking the position of the axle

37 (1½ in)

6 mm (¼ in)

xxx keep these edges flush

a

b

Figure 232 *Below* Using a template to locate the handle-fixing screws in the upright

keep edges sharp

Figure 231 Rounding the corners of the sides

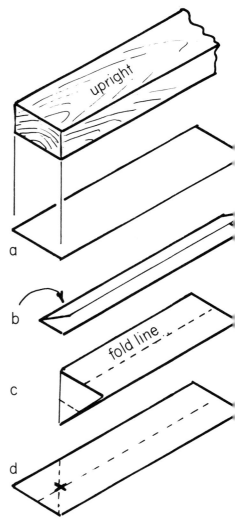

upright

fold line

a

b

c

d

Move inwards 37 mm (1½ in) along this line from each end to find the axle drilling position.

To provide a lead to the drill, a nail should be hammered into this position until its point has just entered, and then it should be removed.

Both sides should now be drilled together to save further measuring (Figure 230b). While doing this be *very* careful to keep the drill vertical or you will meet problems later on.

Drill with a 6 mm (¼ in) diameter bit.

2 Round off the corners of the sides.

This procedure is essential as sharp corners and young children do not mix.

Use a small round egg-cup or wine glass — you do not want to take off too much — and surform to the marked line. There is likely to be little material to remove, so it is hardly worthwhile sawing off the bulk (Figure 231).

Remember, you are only rounding off the corners, not chamfering the edges. Keep edges sharp until construction is complete.

3 The handle is fixed to the upright by means of two screws (item 7) through the uprights.

The positions of these screws should be found using a template to keep them in the same position and prevent the handle from looking askew.

The template is shown in Figure 232a-d.

Take a strip of paper the same width as the upright (Figure 232a).

Fold over along its length and unfold (Figure 232b).

Fold one end across diagonally, and unfold (Figure 232c).

Mark the point where the fold lines cross. This is the drilling position (Figure 232d).

4 Position the template on the upright, and using a sharp pencil or a nail, mark the hole position through on to the wood (Figure 233a).

Drill the hole with a 5 mm ($\frac{3}{16}$ in) diameter drill (Figure 233b).

The top corners of each upright should now be rounded off as described in operation 2 (Figure 233c).

5 The sides are fixed to the base and ends with glue and 37 mm ($1\frac{1}{2}$ in) oval brad nails. To find the position of these nails, the profile of the base and end on each side must be found. A method of doing this is illustrated in Figure 234a-b.

Draw lines *A* and *B* touching the edges of the axle holes at 90° to the lower edge of the side (Figure 234a).

Now use the width of one of the ends to mark the profile (Figure 234a). The profile is shown shaded in Figure 234b.

Along the middle of this shaded area, hammer in eleven 37 mm ($1\frac{1}{2}$ in) brad nails, as indicated in Figure 234b, until the points of the nails can just be felt, coming through the other side of the wood.

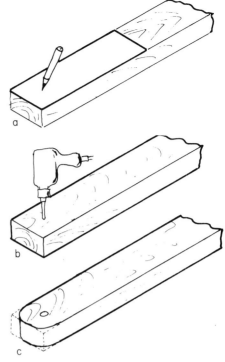

Figure 233 Marking the screw hold positions, drilling the holes and rounding the corners

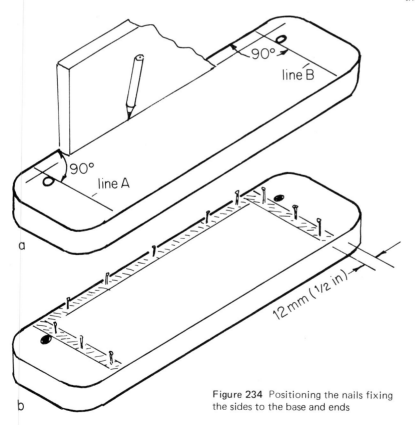

Figure 234 Positioning the nails fixing the sides to the base and ends

131

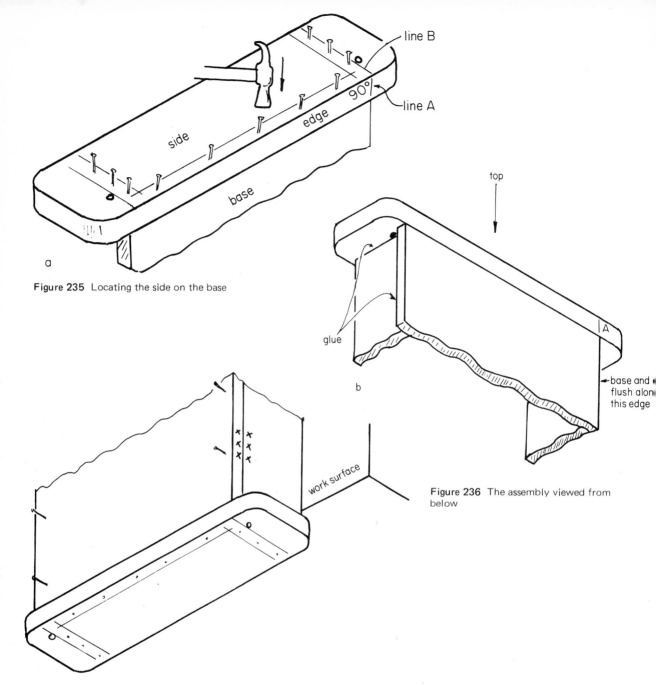

Figure 235 Locating the side on the base

a

b

Figure 236 The assembly viewed from below

line B

line A

90°

side

edge

base

top

glue

A

base and ◄
flush alon
this edge

work surface

6 Mark line A, extending the base profile line on item 1 (side) from the face to the edge (Figure 235a).

Rest the base on its edge on a firm surface (you will need help to do this). Apply glue and position the side.

The base should line up with line A at one end. At the other end, it will stick out a bit further (Figure 236a).

Hammer the nails into the base.

Punch the nails below the surface.

Wipe off excess glue.

If you find that any nails fail to go right into the wood, but bend slightly and stick out of the side, do not attempt to remove them until the glue has thoroughly set.

132

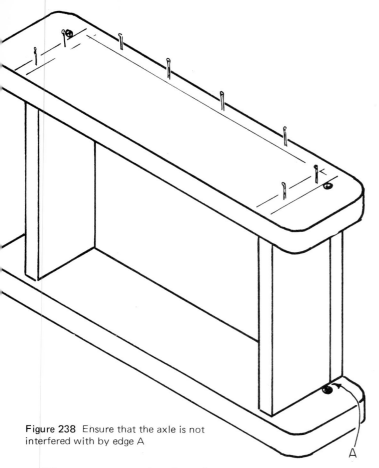

Figure 238 Ensure that the axle is not interfered with by edge A

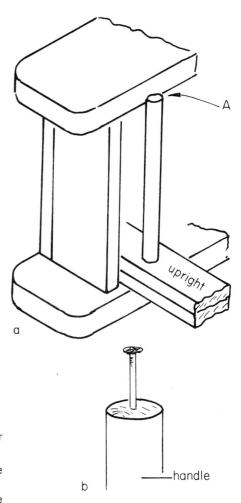

Figure 239 Checking the length of the dowelling used for the handle

Whenever you see that the nails are going wrong just ignore them for the time being.

7 Working at the same angle as for operation 6 the ends should now be glued and nailed in position.

Remember to apply glue along the edge where the base meets the end.

Make sure that *both* ends touch the edge of the axle hole, at the same time, allowing the axle to fit through freely.

Along one edge, the base and end should be flush at area *xxx* (Figure 237).

At the other end, the base will stick out a bit. This is not a cause for concern unless it sticks out beyond the profile of the actual side.

Hammer home the nails in the side and then fix the base to the end (Figure 237) using as few 25 mm (1 in) nails as possible. Three per joint is about the right number.

8 Now glue and position the other side. Make sure that the axles have free access in all of the holes and are not interfered with by edge A (see Figure 238).

Check that the side and the base are flush along the bottom edge.

Hammer home all the nails.

Punch nail-heads below the surface.

Wipe off excess glue.

9 If the length of 25 mm (1 in) dowel available for the handle is the length suggested in the materials list, it should be just about right with no cutting required. Check this as shown in Figure 239a.

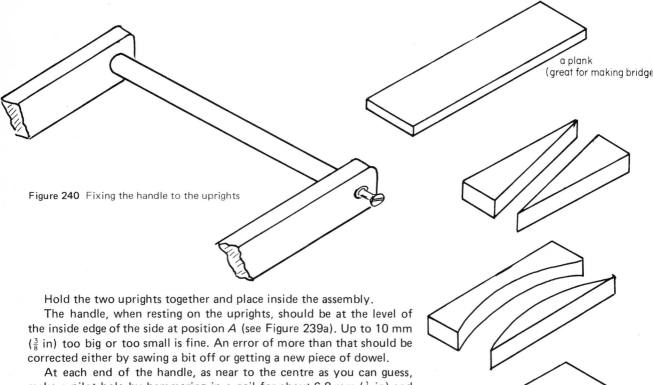

a plank
(great for making bridge

Figure 240 Fixing the handle to the uprights

Hold the two uprights together and place inside the assembly.

The handle, when resting on the uprights, should be at the level of the inside edge of the side at position *A* (see Figure 239a). Up to 10 mm ($\frac{3}{8}$ in) too big or too small is fine. An error of more than that should be corrected either by sawing a bit off or getting a new piece of dowel.

At each end of the handle, as near to the centre as you can guess, make a pilot hole by hammering in a nail for about 6-8 mm ($\frac{1}{4}$ in) and then removing it (Figure 239b).

10 Apply glue liberally to the end of the handle and fix the handle to the uprights with 37 mm ($1\frac{1}{2}$ in) No. 8 screws and cupwashers (see Figure 240).

Before the glue sets, the uprights should be glued and nailed with two nails per upright to the body of the truck.

The uprights should have glue applied to their ends and should be hand-held firmly into the inside corner of the baby-walker, then the 37 mm ($1\frac{1}{2}$ in) oval brads should be hammered in from the inside.

Finish and varnish (see Finishing, page 20).

Fit the axles and wheels. The axles supplied may be too long, in which case they will have to be shortened with a hack-saw.

You will certainly be able to borrow a hack-saw from some friend or other.

Bricks

11 Commercial children's play bricks are about as imaginatively made as prison porridge. Each set of bricks should give the child a lesson in shape, form, and fitting.

You should be able to pick up wood off-cuts very cheaply — perhaps even free — and, using your imagination, you will be able to fill the baby-walker to overflowing with material for hours of gloriously silent play.

Some of the shapes suggested in Figure 241 require the use of a jig-saw attachment for an electric drill.

Remember that these items are likely to be chewed so you *must* make sure that all the corners and edges are meticulously smoothed, and that the surface coating which you decide to use is both lead-free and non-toxic.

Figure 241 Some suggested brick shapes

Project 17

STILTS

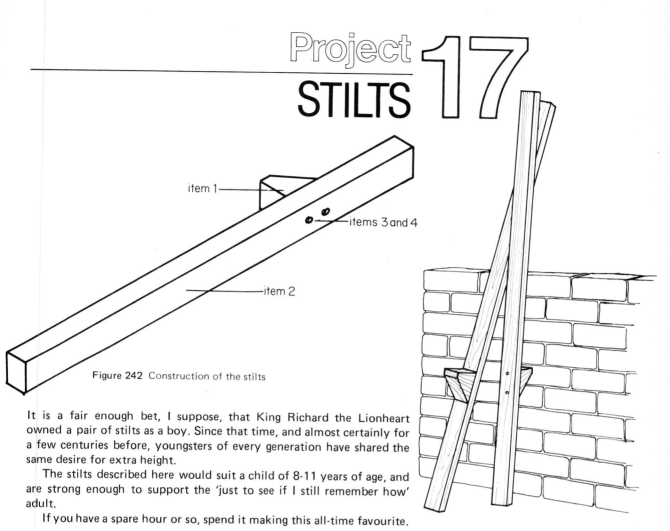

item 1

items 3 and 4

item 2

Figure 242 Construction of the stilts

It is a fair enough bet, I suppose, that King Richard the Lionheart owned a pair of stilts as a boy. Since that time, and almost certainly for a few centuries before, youngsters of every generation have shared the same desire for extra height.

The stilts described here would suit a child of 8-11 years of age, and are strong enough to support the 'just to see if I still remember how' adult.

If you have a spare hour or so, spend it making this all-time favourite.

Materials

Item no.	Description	Quantity
1	dressed pine 70 x 45 x 150 mm (3 x 2 nom x 6 in)	1
2	dressed pine 45 mm x 35 mm x 1.650 m (2 in x 1½ in nom x 5 ft 6 in)	2
3	countersunk wood screws 50 mm (2 in) x No. 8	4
4	No. 8 cup washers	4
	PVA woodworker's adhesive	
	glass or garnet paper (medium)	1 sheet
	varnish to finish	

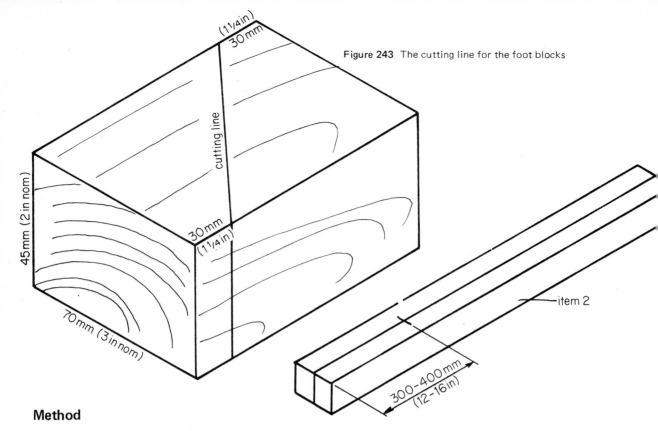

Figure 243 The cutting line for the foot blocks

Figure 244 Positioning the foot blocks

Method

1 First make the feet blocks. Both of these are cut from the same piece of timber (item 1).

Mark a point 30 mm ($1\frac{1}{4}$ in) along the side of the block from one corner. Repeat this for the diagonally opposite corner. Join the points to mark the cutting line (Figure 243).

A bench hook (see Tools, page 11) will help to hold the block firmly while you are sawing it, but such a small piece of timber as this is always difficult to hold, so go carefully.

The sawn surface should be smoothed with glass or garnet paper before fixing the blocks to the uprights.

Unless you have a vice, you can best do this by holding the sheet of abrasive paper face up on a flat surface and rubbing the foot block back and forth on it, with the cut surface downwards.

2 You are now ready to position the foot blocks.

Hold both uprights together (see Figure 244) with the 45 mm (2 in nom) edge (the widest one) uppermost. Mark both uprights together 300-400 mm (12 in-16 in) from the end. This mark shows the position of the top of the foot blocks. If you are unsure of the actual safe height for the youngster in question, set the block position high, rather than low. It will be easy to reduce the height on the finished articles by sawing small equal pieces off each stilt.

3 From the line you have just marked you can work out the clearance hole positions for the foot block fixing screws as shown in Figure 245. The dimensions shown are approximate. Drill through with a 4.5 mm ($\frac{5}{16}$ in) drill.

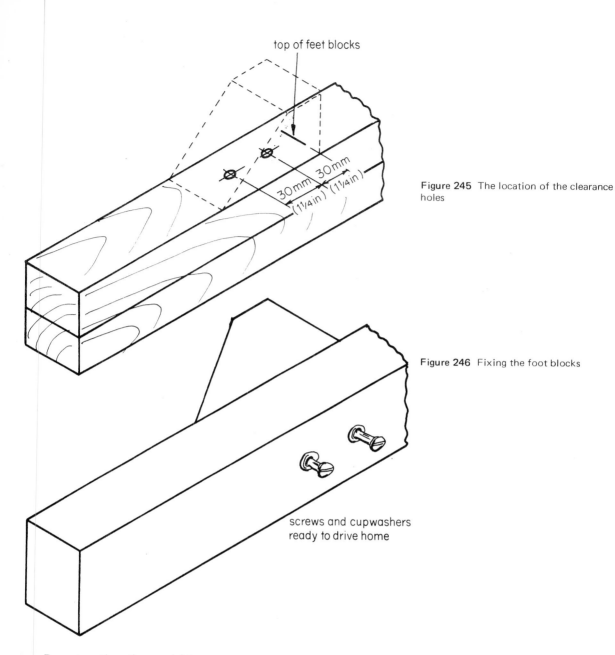

top of feet blocks

30mm 30mm
(1¼in) (1¼in)

Figure 245 The location of the clearance holes

Figure 246 Fixing the foot blocks

screws and cupwashers
ready to drive home

Repeat on the other upright.

The dotted lines indicate the final position of the foot block.

4 Screw and glue.

Half hammer, half screw (see Screwing, page 15) the feet blocks to the uprights, making sure that the top of the foot block is on the line marked in Figure 246.

Remove all sharp or rough edges with medium grade glass paper, and varnish finish (see Finishing, page 19).

Project 18
SLEDGE

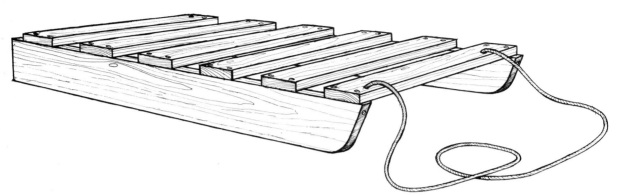

To the very best of my knowledge, all family carpenters are keen tobogganists. The first whisper of snow and it is into the garage (for the lucky ones) to revive that rotting relic of childhood — the family sledge. Lacking even this, the best you can do is take a walk in the park to watch other people and their children having a ball.

Do not be caught out next winter, since this item is so easy to make, and would be greatly appreciated as a child's Christmas present.

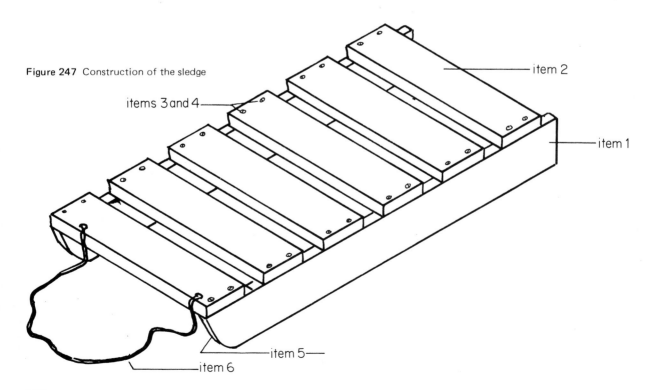

Figure 247 Construction of the sledge

items 3 and 4

item 2

item 1

item 5

item 6

Materials

Item no.	Description	Quantity
1	red or white pine 95 x 20 x 1800 mm (4 in x 1 in nom x 6 ft)	1
2	red or white pine 95 x 20 x 400 mm (4 in x 1 in nom x 1 ft 4 in)	6
3	37 mm ($1\frac{1}{2}$ in) x No. 8 brass countersunk screws	24
4	No. 8 brass (or brassed) cup washers	24
5*	Aluminium alloy or steel 25 mm wide x 2 mm x 1 m long (1 in wide x $\frac{3}{16}$ in thick x 3 ft 4 in long)	2
	25 mm (1 in) No. 6 steel screws to suit	approx 20
6	6 mm ($\frac{1}{4}$ in) diameter polypropylene rope or clothes-line	2 m (7 ft)
7 (not shown in Fig. 16)	quarter-round hardwood beading 25 x 25 mm (1 x 1 in)	1.2 m (4 ft)
8	'one-shot' waterproof wood glue	as re-quired

*Aluminium alloy, although slightly more expensive, is easier to bend and drill, and does not rust.

Method

1 Item 1 is used to make the runners (Figure 248).
   Take the 1800 mm (6 ft) length (item 1) and mark the centre line. Item 1 may not be exactly 1800 mm (6 ft) long so you should measure it and halve this measurement to find the exact position of the centre line. Then mark the cutting line as shown in Figure 249.

Figure 249 *Left* Marking out the curve on item 1

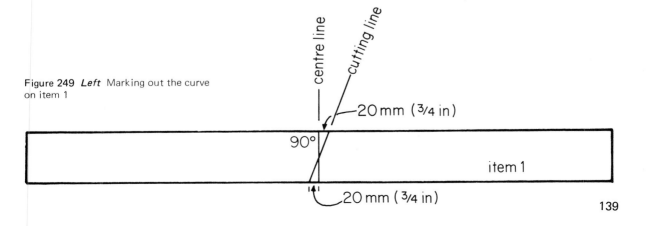

139

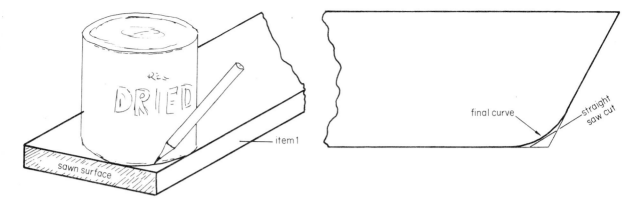

Figure 250 *Above* Cutting the curve on item 1 — start with a straight saw cut

2 Saw item 1 along the cutting line by supporting the material on a bench hook (see Tools, page 11).

Mark a curve on this cutting line by drawing round some circular object which has a diameter of about 100 mm (4 in), e.g. a cup or food can (Figure 249).

3 As much as possible of the curve should be removed by one straight saw cut (Figure 250). Surform to the final curved shape (see surforming, page 20).

Repeat operations 1-3 for the second runner.

4 Make a drilling template for the screw positions on items 2 (the top slats). Take a strip of paper 95 mm (4 in nom) wide, i.e. slat width, and mark a 20 mm (1 in nom) strip at one end using one of the top slats (item 2) (see Figure 251a).

Fold the 20 mm (1 in nom) strip in half, then unfold (Figure 251b).

Fold corners over to the pencil line, and mark the drilling positions at the point where the edge of the paper meets the previous fold line as indicated in Figure 252.

5 Using the template, mark the hole positions at each end of the slats (item 2) and drill through on to waste wood with a 4.5 mm ($\frac{3}{16}$ in) drill (Figure 253).

Repeat this operation for all six slats.

6 Holding the runners (item 1) together, mark on both runners at once, all six slat positions.

Lay one slat across the runners at the forwardmost position and mark with a pencil (Figure 254a).

Remove this slat, and mark a 50 mm (2 in) gap. Replace the slat and mark the next slat position (Figure 254b). Repeat until all the six slat positions have been marked.

7 Fixing the slats to the runners is really a two-man job, since the slats have to be held in position as they are being glued and screwed. When using brass screws, it normally helps to rub the screw thread with ordinary household soap, as this makes it easier to drive the screw home.

Using the half hammer — half screw method (see Screwing, page 15) fix one slat at a time (Figure 255).

'One-shot' waterproof wood glue should be used and do not forget to put the cup washers under the screws.

8 Cut item 7, the hardwood beading, into twelve lengths each about 80 mm (3 in) long. These will be used as glue blocks to strengthen the slat/runner joints. Apply cascamite to the adjacent faces of the block. Position these faces against the slat/runner corner (Figure 256) and rub

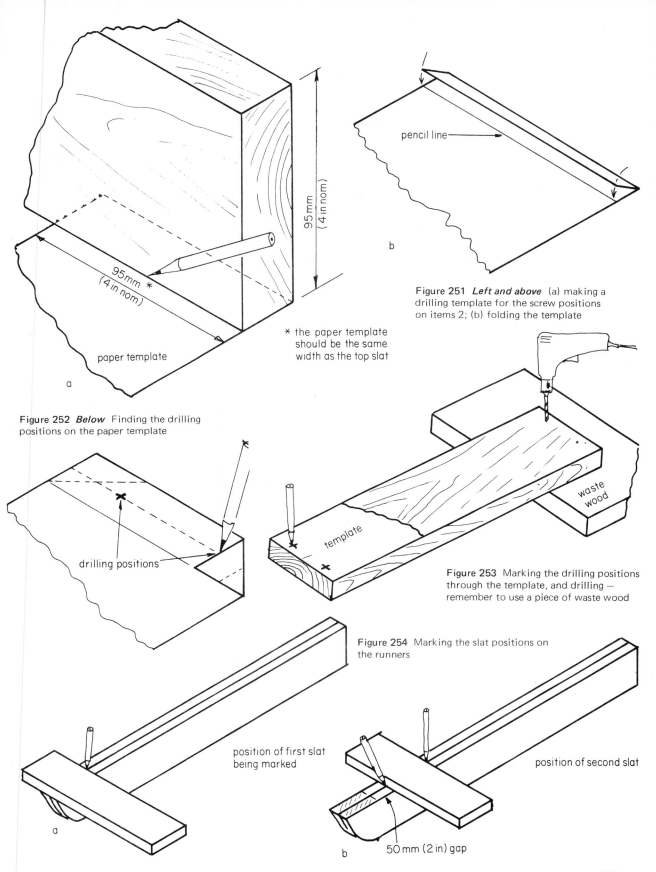

95mm (4 in nom)

95mm (4 in nom) *

* the paper template should be the same width as the top slat

paper template

a

pencil line

b

Figure 251 *Left and above* (a) making a drilling template for the screw positions on items 2; (b) folding the template

Figure 252 *Below* Finding the drilling positions on the paper template

drilling positions

template

waste wood

Figure 253 Marking the drilling positions through the template, and drilling — remember to use a piece of waste wood

Figure 254 Marking the slat positions on the runners

position of first slat being marked

a

position of second slat

b

50 mm (2 in) gap

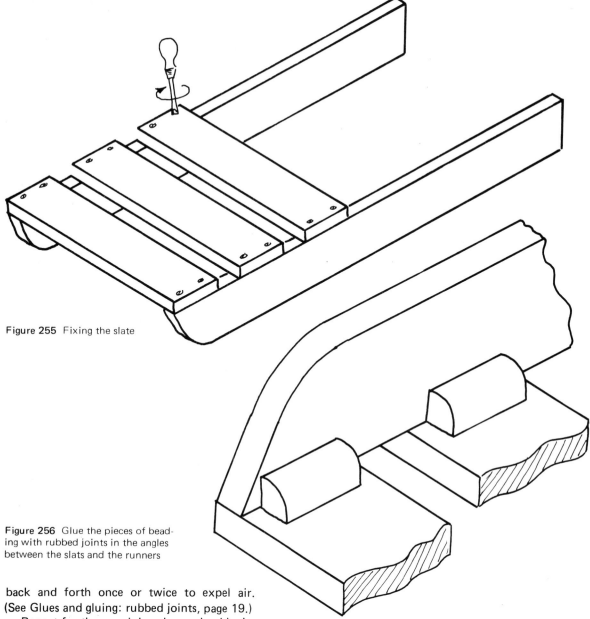

Figure 255 Fixing the slate

Figure 256 Glue the pieces of beading with rubbed joints in the angles between the slats and the runners

back and forth once or twice to expel air. (See Glues and gluing: rubbed joints, page 19.)

Repeat for the remaining eleven glue blocks.

9 Check that the length of aluminium alloy runner that you have purchased is not too long.

Drill and countersink the aluminium alloy or steel runner in ten positions to suit the No. 6 x 25 mm (1 in) fixing screws (see Drilling, page 18). Mark two drilling positions 20 mm ($\frac{3}{4}$ in) in from each end of the runner, then equally space the other eight drilling positions along the length of the runner.

Repeat the drilling and countersinking operation for the second runner.

Screw the metal strip to the runners.

10 Drill two 6 mm ($\frac{1}{4}$ in) holes in the front slat for the tow rope.

11 Finish with three coats of gloss varnish (see Finishing, page 21).

Now it can snow when it likes!

GO-CART 19

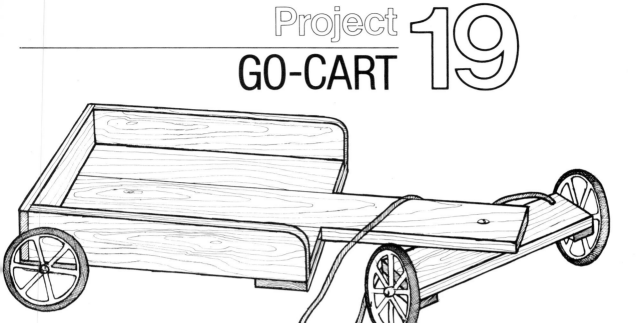

With increasing affluence over the past ten to twenty years many features of our culture have faded away almost to vanishing point.

I refer in particular to the late lamented 'cartie', 'bogie', 'guider', 'gig' . . . the names being as varied and colourful as the designs themselves.

The styles were very dependant on the availability of local (free) materials, each source being tapped almost to exhaustion, regardless of any conventional laws of ownership.

Against that background, this model is very much a second-class citizen, but your children will not know that — they will love it!

Materials

Item no.	Description	Quantity
1	dressed pine 95 x 20 x 450 mm (4 x 1 nom x 18 in)	4
2	dressed pine 95 x 20 x 350 mm (4 x 1 nom x 14 in)	4
3 and 4	150 mm (6 in) diameter plastic wheels	4
	450 mm (18 in) axle 9 mm ($\frac{3}{8}$ in) diameter + spring end caps	2
5	9 mm ($\frac{3}{8}$ in) diameter, 60 mm ($2\frac{1}{2}$ in) long slotted-head screws, nuts, and washers	3 of each

Item no.	Description	Quantity
6 and **7**	dressed pine 45 mm x 20 mm x 1.2 m (2 in x 1 in nom x 4 ft)	1
8	dressed pine 95 x 20 x 750 mm (4 in x 1 in x 2 ft 6 in)	1
	PVA woodworker's adhesive	
	37 mm ($1\frac{1}{2}$ in) oval brad nails	30 approx
	37 mm ($1\frac{1}{2}$ in) x No. 8 countersunk-head screws	6
9	Rope (for brakes and steering)	3 m (10 ft)

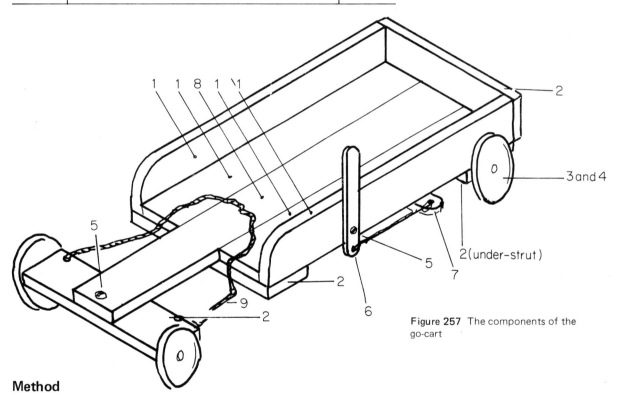

Figure 257 The components of the go-cart

Method

1 To curve the forward corner of the side (item 1), you need a tin can of diameter 70–150 mm (3–6 in). Place it on one corner of the side and draw round it (Figure 258a). With one straight saw cut (Figure 258b) remove as much material as possible and then surform down to the required curve.

Repeat this on the other side.

2 The next task is fixing the two under-struts (item 2) on to one side.

Mark on both struts together a line showing the width of the side (Figure 259a).

144

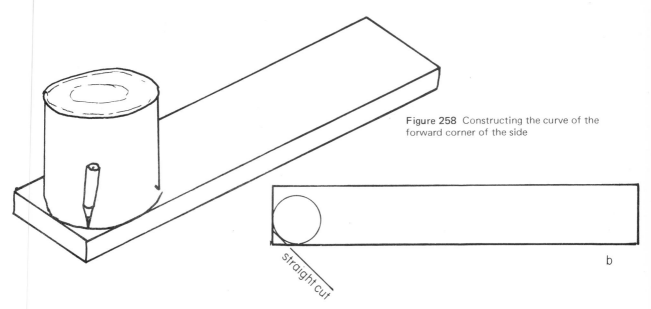

Figure 258 Constructing the curve of the forward corner of the side

straight cut

b

Along the centre (approximately) of this strip draw another straight line (line *A* on Figure 259b) and, at the centre of this line hammer in a 37 mm (1½ in) oval brad nail until the tip just protrudes through the strut.

Apply glue on the area of the side where the joints will be made, and drive the single nail home in each of the two under-struts, after ensuring that all the edges marked *x* in Figure 259b are flush.

Using your square (see Tools, page 10) check that the angles marked 90° in Figure 259b are in fact 90°.

Along the same nail line (line *A* Figure 259b) drive a pair of nails home into each strut in dovetail fashion (Figure 259c) and punch them below the surface (see Nailing, page 15). This nail-punching is not for appearance, but safety. Remember — this is a toy!

3 The floor spars, 2 short (item 1) and 1 long (item 8), are fixed to the under-struts with glue and a single 37 mm (1½ in) No. 8 screw at each end of the floor spars.

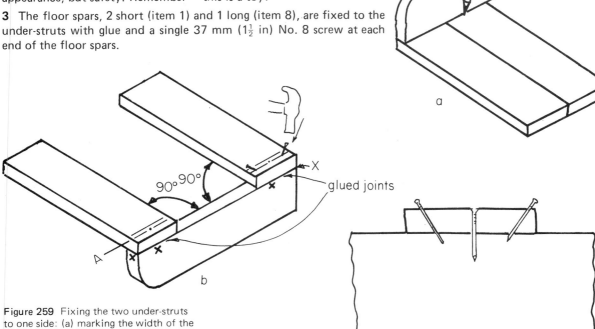

90° 90°

X

glued joints

A

b

a

c

Figure 259 Fixing the two under-struts to one side: (a) marking the width of the side; (b) gluing the sides; (c) nailing the sides dovetail fashion to the struts

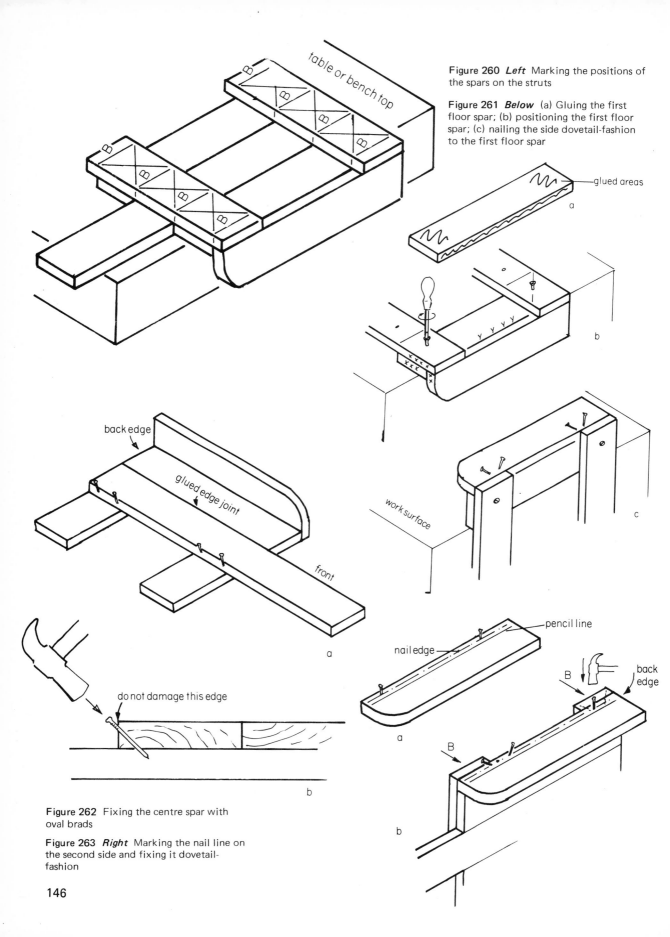

table or bench top

Figure 260 *Left* Marking the positions of the spars on the struts

Figure 261 *Below* (a) Gluing the first floor spar; (b) positioning the first floor spar; (c) nailing the side dovetail-fashion to the first floor spar

glued areas

a

b

work surface

c

back edge

glued edge joint

front

a

do not damage this edge

b

pencil line

nail edge

a

B

back edge

B

b

Figure 262 Fixing the centre spar with oval brads

Figure 263 *Right* Marking the nail line on the second side and fixing it dovetail-fashion

146

The screw is screwed through the under-struts into the spars and to fix its position it is necessary to find the actual position of the floor spars on the struts.

Working on the edge of a bench or table, place the floor spars in position.

Looking down from above and using a ruler you can mark the positions of the spars on the struts (lines marked *B* in Figure 260).

Cross the diagonals of the rectangles formed by the lines *B* on the under-struts. The points where they cross are the positions through which you drill the 5 mm ($\frac{3}{16}$ in) diameter clearance holes for the No. 8 screws.

This is done on the same table top after removing the floor spars. For this operation, remember to cover the table with a fairly thick piece of waste wood, to avoid damaging your work surface.

4   Apply glue to the first floor spar as indicated in Figure 261a.

Position the glued floor spar and make sure that the edges are flush in the area marked *xxx* (Figure 261b).

Also pull the spar against the side to close the gap marked with *Y*s.

Now half hammer, half screw (see Screwing, page 15) the two 37 mm ($1\frac{1}{2}$ in) No. 8 screws until they are about half a turn from home.

Invert the job on the work surface (Figure 261c) and fix the side to the floor spar by hammering in four 37 mm ($1\frac{1}{2}$ in) oval brads in dove-tail fashion (see Figure 261c).

Nail-punch the heads below the surface.

Note: if when hammering the nail into the side and floor spar, you find that the point is coming out of the side, leave the nail as it is and try again with a new nail. When the glue has fully set, the first nail can be removed with the hammer claw without moving the freshly glued pieces.

Now return to the screws and drive them fully home.

The clearance hole into which they are fitted is of such a size as to allow the screw heads to be driven flush with the surface without too much effort.

Wipe off excess glue.

5   Then position the centre floor slat.

Apply glue along the edge of the first floor spar and on the areas of the under-strut which will be in contact with the centre (long) floor slat, and place the centre spar in position (Figure 262a).

Make sure that the long edge is sticking out at the front of the cart, and that the back edges of the spars and the under-strut are flush.

The 37 mm ($1\frac{1}{2}$ in) oval brads shown in Figure 262 are meant to pull the edges up tight and should therefore be hammered in at a fairly shallow angle (see Figure 262b). Drive the nails under the surface using a nail-punch.

Now invert the job and half hammer, half screw in the two No. 8 screws which fix the floor spar to the under-strut.

Drive the screws flush with the surface.

Wipe off excess glue.

Fix the third floor spar in exactly the same way.

6   Using the edge of a piece of 95 mm x 20 mm (4 in x 1 in nom) section timber as a guide, mark on the outside of the second side, a pencil line 20 mm (1 in nom) from the lower edge (Figure 263a).

Draw a line along the centre of this strip. This is the nail line for fixing the side to the base.

About 50 mm (2 in) from each end of this nail line, hammer in a

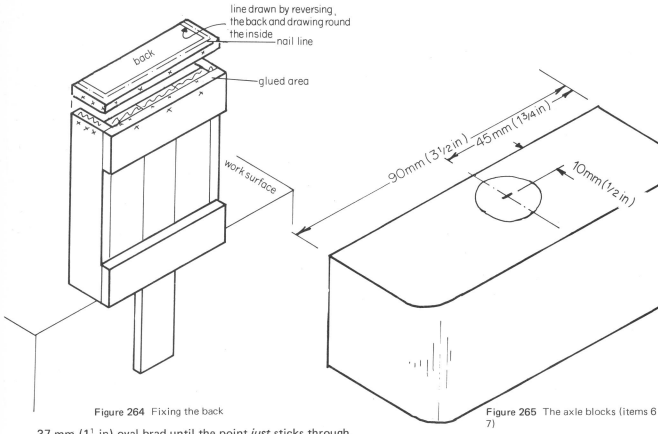

line drawn by reversing the back and drawing round the inside

nail line

back

glued area

work surface

Figure 264 Fixing the back

Figure 265 The axle blocks (items 6 7)

37 mm (1½ in) oval brad until the point *just* sticks through.

Apply glue to the edge of the last base spar and the under-strut, and position the side.

Make sure that all edges are flush along the back edge and that the side is hard against the under-struts. The nail points sticking through should hold it in position. Hammer these two nails home and fix four nails in dovetail fashion along the nail line (Figure 263b).

Lay the assembly upside down on the work surface and fix each underspar to the side with two dovetailed 37 mm (1½ in) oval brads. Wipe off excess glue.

The under-struts will probably stick out slightly. This can be remedied after the back has been put on and the glue has set by sawing and surforming, or simply surforming them flush to the side.

7 First make sure that the back is the correct width to fit flush at the edges as indicated in Figure 264.

If it is only about 3 mm ($\frac{1}{8}$ in) too long, leave it for the moment and surform it flush as part of the finishing operation.

At this stage you may wish to mark and surform a small radius (egg-cup size) on the top corners of the back. This is optional.

The back is held to the body with glue and nails.

To find the nail line (marked with dashes and dots on Figure 264) simply reverse the back and place it in position. Mark the contact area in pencil. The nail line is at the approximate centre of this strip.

Apply glue to the body (as indicated in Figure 264) and position the back, keeping it flush along the edges marked *X*. It is unlikely to be flush at both edges, so make sure that it is flush along at least one side.

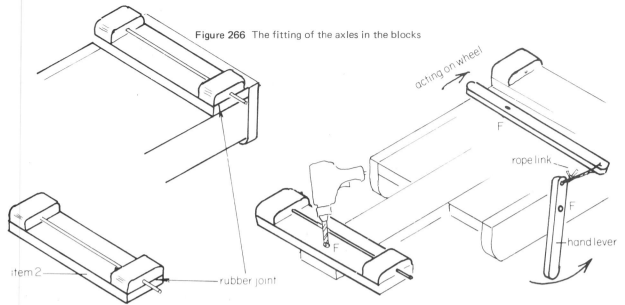

Figure 266 The fitting of the axles in the blocks

item 2 — rubber joint

Figure 267 The steering and braking arrangements

acting on wheel

rope link

hand lever

Now fix the back to the body using about six to eight 37 mm ($1\frac{1}{2}$ in) oval brads, hammered in vertically around the nail line. Do not bother with dovetail nailing unless the back is slightly warped and the glue joint will not close.

Wipe off excess glue and lay aside for the glue to dry.

Once the glue is dry, surform, or saw and surform the back making it flush with the sides.

8 Cut four blocks each 90 mm ($3\frac{1}{2}$ in) long from the length purchased for items 6 and 7.

The corners may be rounded if you wish as shown in Figure 265. The centre of the 9 mm ($\frac{3}{8}$ in) axle hole should be marked as indicated. A nail may be hammered into this position just past its tip to give the drill an accurate centre, thus avoiding 'wander'.

Drill through in this position with a 9 mm ($\frac{3}{8}$ in) diameter drill.

Ask someone to hold the block steady on a piece of waste wood so that you can concentrate on drilling as vertically as possible.

Repeat this procedure for all four blocks.

9 The 9 mm ($\frac{3}{8}$ in) diameter axles fit into these blocks as shown in Figure 266.

The blocks are glued to the steering strut (item 2) and to the rear under-strut with the axle in position: this avoids any difficulties caused by misalignment.

Glue is applied to the underside of the blocks and a rubbed joint is made with the blocks in position as shown in Figure 266 (see Joints, page 19).

This joint must be left for at least 3-4 hours before it can be handled or the axle safely removed.

10 Finally the steering strut and brake are fitted.

The steering strut is laid across the front of the centre floor spar as shown in Figure 267 and a 9 mm ($\frac{3}{8}$ in) diameter hole (F) is drilled in the centre at some point in front of the axle (see Figure 267). Line this up by eye. Bolt the steering strut into place.

The braking system shown in Figure 267 is, I think, self-explanatory, and the positions marked *F*, through which the 9 mm ($\frac{3}{8}$ in) nuts and screws hold the brake levers to the chassis, are best found by trial and error.

This brake design was suggested by a friend who was raised in Edinburgh. He thought that the rope link gave a sense of remote control, which used to please him.

I would not think that this is the only possible way to stop a machine of this type, and if you have a favourite method, use it.

Finish and varnish or paint (see Finishing, page 19). And what about a name?

Whizz? Hurricane? . . .

Project 20
EASEL

Children love to draw and paint. I think that in general we reach the age of about twelve or thirteen years of age before some of us sadly realise that we are only of average artistic ability and hence lose interest in the subject.

Before that fateful age is reached, there is no such spirit of competition and art really is for art's sake. Children create because their instincts tell them to.

We for our part can only provide them with encouragement. By making an easel and blackboard such as the one described here, and providing them with some of the basic materials, we can allow them to express their creative talents.

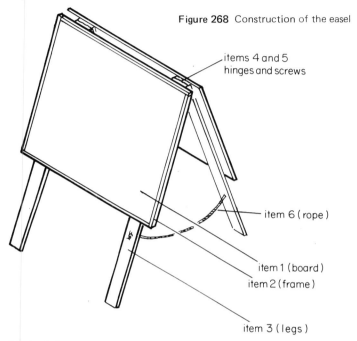

Figure 268 Construction of the easel

items 4 and 5
hinges and screws

item 6 (rope)

item 1 (board)
item 2 (frame)

item 3 (legs)

Materials

Item no.	Description	Quantity
1	12 mm ($\frac{1}{2}$ in) chipboard (particle board) 600 x 450 mm (2 ft x 1 ft 6 in)	2
2	12 x 12 mm ($\frac{1}{2}$ in) hardwood beading 5 m (15 ft)	1
3	dressed pine 95 mm x 20 mm x 1 m (4 in x 1 in nom x 3 ft 6 in)	4
4 and 5	brassed butt hinges 75 mm (3 in) + fixing screws	2
6	rope 5 mm ($\frac{1}{4}$ in) diameter approx $1\frac{1}{2}$ m (5 ft) long	1
	PVA woodworker's adhesive	
	25 mm (1 in) oval brads	50 approx
	30 mm ($1\frac{1}{4}$ in) x No. 6 countersunk wood screws	16

Item no.	Description		Quantity
	blackboard paint (or matt-black paint)		
	white emulsion paint		
	white gloss paint		
	glass or garnet paper	medium smooth	1 sheet 1 sheet

Method

1 First prepare the surfaces. One surface will be black, the other white. The reverse side of each board may be left untreated.

At this stage, handle the boards gently as unprotected chipboard (particle board) corners break easily and it will be quite difficult to hide these blemishes later on.

Prepare a thin mixture of cellulose-based plaster-type crack-filler, e.g. Pollyfilla. Spread this mixture as thinly as possible over the *smooth* side of each chipboard sheet (one side will be slightly smoother than the other) and leave to dry in a warm place overnight. The surface can then be rubbed down with medium glass or garnet paper thus giving a smooth surface on which the paint can be applied.

Try to keep the edges clean as the hardwood framing will have to be nailed and glued to them, and glue sticks best to clean material.

Paint each smoothed surface with white emulsion paint and leave overnight. Next day rub down with smooth glass or garnet paper.

Clean dust off the surfaces with a lightly dampened cloth and work-ing in as dust-free a room as you can find (or are allowed to work in!) paint one surface with blackboard (or matt black) paint and the other with white gloss.

The white painted surface *may* need a light rub down with smooth sand-paper followed by a second coat of gloss, but the blackboard should be all right as it is.

2 The hardwood framing serves a dual purpose by enhancing the appearance of the chipboard and protecting its weak edges.

The method of fixing the framing shown in Figure 269 is recom-mended because it entirely eliminates the need for accurate measure-ment. If you would prefer to use any other method, then by all means go ahead — the function will be unaltered.

Working with the chipboard on the floor, perhaps supported by a helper, apply glue to the edge, hold the framing in position, and fix with five or six 25 mm (1 in) oval brads (Figure 269). Punch the nail heads below the surface (see Nailing, page 15).

Ensure that the edges marked *xxx* in the figure are flush. This check is most important as any finishing work necessary on the frame may damage the pre-prepared surface, which will be difficult to repair with-out getting paint on the hardwood frame.

Wipe off excess glue.

3 The remaining three pieces of framing are glued and nailed in a similar fashion checking in each case that the edge of the framing, and

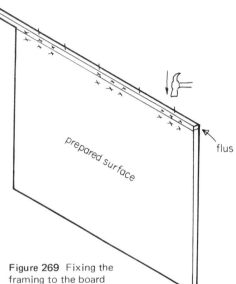

prepared surface

flus

Figure 269 Fixing the framing to the board

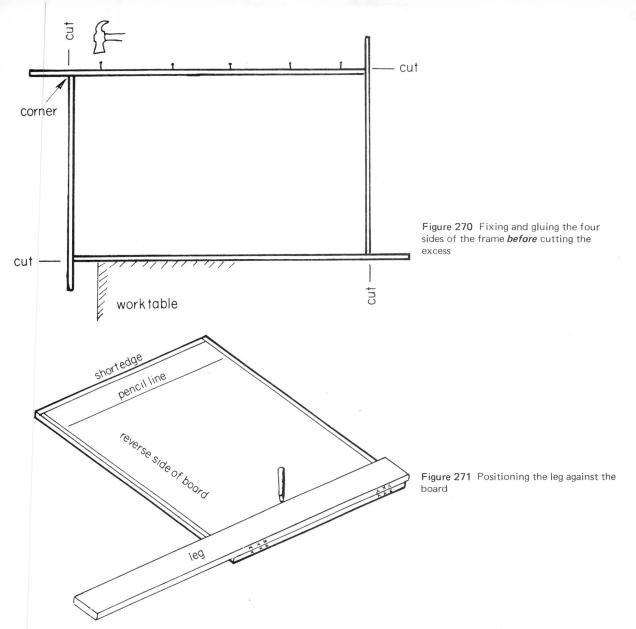

Figure 270 Fixing and gluing the four sides of the frame **before** cutting the excess

Figure 271 Positioning the leg against the board

the prepared surface, are flush and that the frame is pushed well into the corner giving a close joint at that point (see Figure 270).

The last piece of framing must be fixed, with the board on an elevated work surface. This may make nailing a little more tricky, but do not let your work suffer. If you are having trouble, stand on a chair or on the actual work surface, to get yourself in the most comfortable, and hence the best, nailing position.

When the glue is dry (about 3–4 hours) the excess framing at each corner may be sawn off, and the corners slightly rounded with a Surform.

4 Mark the leg positions.

Place one of the legs against the shorter edge of the framed board, and get the edges marked *xxx* flush (Figure 271).

Mark the position of the other edge of the leg on the chipboard (particle board).

Repeat this procedure for both boards.

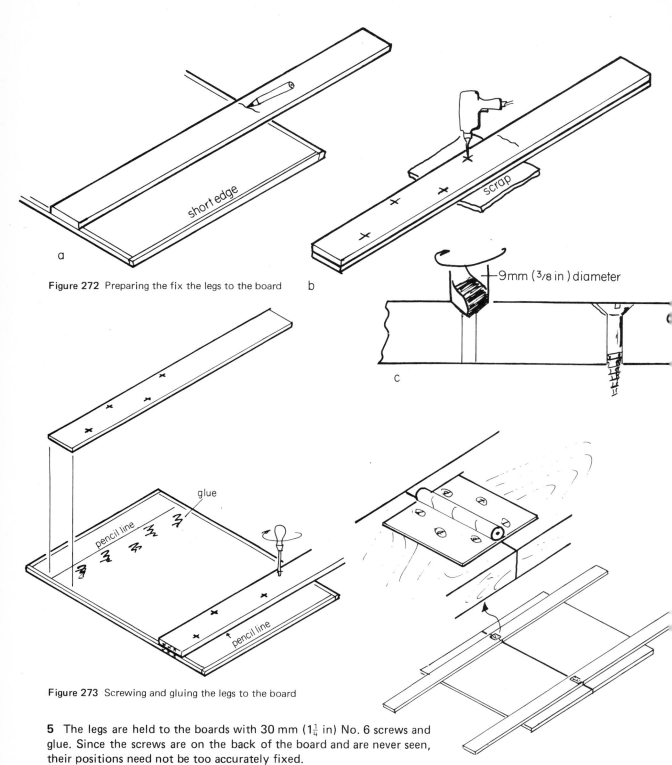

Figure 272 Preparing the fix the legs to the board

a

b

c

—9mm (³⁄8 in) diameter

Figure 273 Screwing and gluing the legs to the board

short edge

scrap

glue

pencil line

pencil line

Figure 274 Fixing the hinges to the board

5 The legs are held to the boards with 30 mm (1$\frac{1}{4}$ in) No. 6 screws and glue. Since the screws are on the back of the board and are never seen, their positions need not be too accurately fixed.

Place the leg as shown in Figure 272 and mark approximately the position of the bottom of the board.

Drill four 3.5 mm ($\frac{1}{8}$ in) diameter holes in a staggered fashion through both legs at once. This saves time. The holes should not be closer than 25 mm (1 in) to any edge, and you should have a piece of

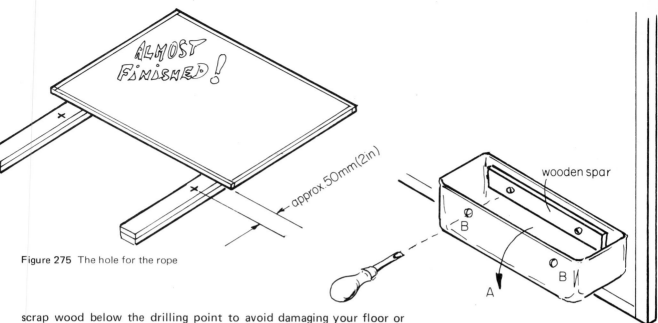

Figure 275 The hole for the rope

Figure 276 A container for chalks, paints ect. If a soft plastic is used, the edge may be pulled down (A) to give screwdriver access

scrap wood below the drilling point to avoid damaging your floor or work surface (Figure 272b).

The holes should now be countersunk by drilling with a 9.5 mm ($\frac{3}{8}$ in) diameter (or largest available) drill until the tip has just entered (Figure 272c). Be very careful here if you are using a power drill, since it can sometimes bite and drill right through of its own accord. If this does happen, just forget about that hole and drill a new one about 10 mm ($\frac{1}{2}$ in) away.

6 Apply some glue to the area that the leg will cover. Since it is such a large area, it is not necessary to cover the whole area. Just squeeze out four or five blobs. These will spread themselves as the screws are tightened.

Position the leg.

Make sure that the edges marked *xxx* in Figure 273 are flush, and that the leg is against the pencil line.

Position the screws and tap them lightly with a hammer to give the thread a start, then drive home fully. Do *not* overtighten.

Repeat for all four legs and wipe off excess glue.

7 Now fit the hinges.

Working on a flat surface, lay out both board assemblies against each other as shown in Figure 274.

Position the 75 mm (3 in) brass or brassed hinge as shown in Figure 274. (Brass looks better, and stands up to moisture a lot better than steel.)

Fixing screws may be provided with the hinge. If not, buy them separately on the advice of your supplier.

These screws should be half hammered, half screwed (see Screwing, page 15) while the hinge is held firmly in position.

8 Rope is fixed through holes positioned as in Figure 275 to ensure that the easel does not open too far and collapse.

Drill holes for the rope (according to the size of the rope purchased) about 50 mm (2 in) down from the lower edge of the board. The rope should be threaded through these holes and knotted at either end. The position of the knots should be fixed by trial and error.

Paper is fixed to the white surface with drawing board clips which are available at any good artist's supply store, but if poster colours are used they can be applied direct to the painted surface, which can later be wiped clean with a damp cloth.

9 As a holder for chalks, paints, etc a plastic container can be fitted to the drawing surface as indicated in Figure 276. This container may be larger if you wish to store dusters, cloths, aprons, and so on.

A wooden spar about 10 mm ($\frac{1}{2}$ in) thick should be used to spread the load of the fixing screws.

If a soft plastic is being used, the edge may be pulled down in the direction of arrow *A* (Figure 261) to allow for screwdriver access. Otherwise, you must drill two holes (position *B* in the figure) so that the screwdriver can get at the screwheads.

Project 21
GLASS CHESSBOARD & BACKGAMMON BOARD, & CHESSMEN

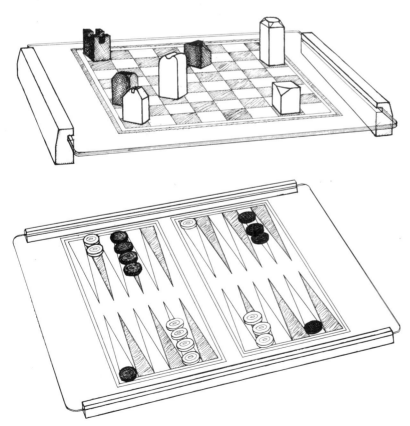

These are not, strictly speaking, purely carpentry projects, but we think that the finished article is too good to be omitted.

A very attractive etched appearance can be obtained by spraying glass with metallic spray paints. The paint is rather fragile, but if it is applied to the underside of the glass surface, there is no reason why it should be scratched.

The instructions are easy to understand, but a sharp fine-bladed knife or scalpel, plus careful measuring, is essential for a truly professional effect.

It is best to use 6 mm ($\frac{1}{4}$ in) thick glass, and to have the edges dressed by the supplier.

Materials

Chessboard
6 mm ($\frac{1}{4}$ in) thick glass 440 x 440 mm (17 x 17 in) all edges dressed

*2 support brackets 250 mm (10 in) long

Backgammon board
6 mm ($\frac{1}{4}$ in) thick glass 510 x 440 mm (1 ft 8$\frac{1}{2}$ in x 1 ft 5$\frac{1}{2}$ in) all edges dressed

*2 support brackets 400 mm (16 in) long

Plus, for both boards
Twin-pack adhesive
hobbyists' gold or silver metallic spray paint
self-adhesive plastic film

*These can be made from hardwood or plastic which is shaped to form the runners for sliding doors.

Figure 277 The layout of the chessboard

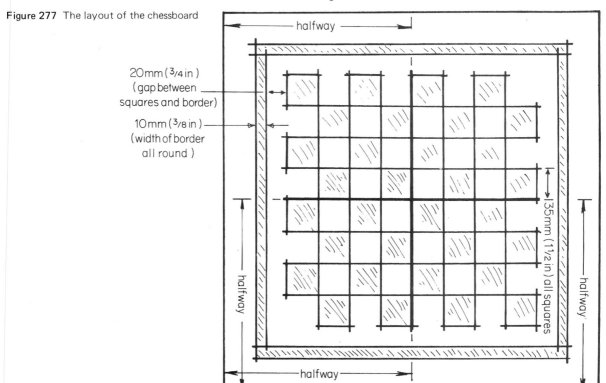

20mm (3/4 in)
(gap between squares and border)

10mm (3/8 in)
(width of border all round)

halfway

135mm (1½ in) all squares

halfway

halfway

halfway

The Boards — Method

1 Cover one side of the sheet of glass with the self-adhesive plastic film, being careful not to trap any large air bubbles between the two.

2 Mark out the desired playing surface on the film surface with a fine-tipped ball-point pen. When you are satisfied that the pattern is correct, go over these ball-pen lines with your sharp-tipped knife. (See Figures 277, 278, and 279.)

You will see in the Figures that the cut lines cross over slightly where they meet. This is intentional since there must be no risk of the cut lines not touching each other.

The glass supplied may not be exactly the size given in the list of materials, but it is important that the playing-boards be centrally positioned on the glass. To ensure this, the cross which marks the centre of the board must be drawn first, by measuring the width of your sheet of glass and halving it. On Figure 277 this cross is shown in double thickness for clarity. You should, of course, draw it with the same fine point that you use for the other lines.

3 The marking for the backgammon board is shown in two figures: Figure 278 shows the details of the rectangles into which the twelve points fit; Figure 279 shows the exact position of the border in relation to the drawing surfaces shown in Figure 278.

4 In all of the figures the shaded area represents the spray-painted area, i.e. the areas of film which are lifted before spraying commences.

Cut along the ball-point lines with a craft knife. To lift the film, push the point of your knife into the centre of a shaded area (as far from the edge as possible) and lift the film with the knife as shown in Figure 280.

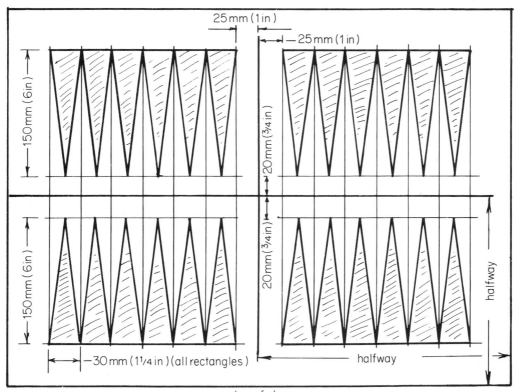

Figure 278
The layout of the backgammon board

edge of glass

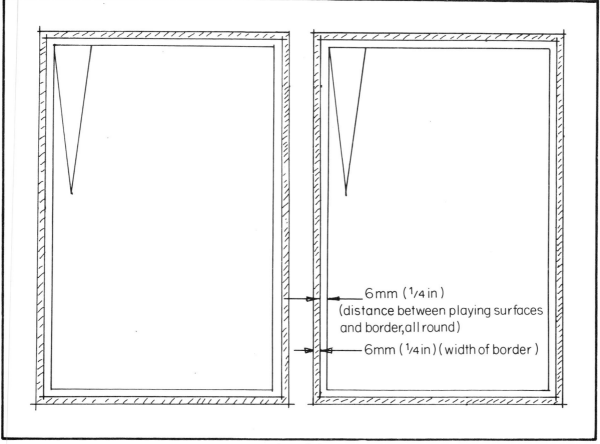

6mm (¼ in)
(distance between playing surfaces
and border, all round)

6mm (¼ in) (width of border)

edge of glass

5 Once all the required areas have been exposed, lightly rub the edge of the remaining film with the back of a spoon. This expels any air bubbles into which paint may spread during the spraying process, thus giving an edge which is not prefectly sharp.

6 Holding the glass sheet vertically, apply three or four light coats of paint according to the instructions on the spray can.

Leave the paint to dry.

Lift off the remaining film as described above.

7 A hobbyist's metallic finish paint is used since the mask can be removed even when the paint has thoroughly dried. With ordinary spray paints, the remaining mask must be removed at a critical point in the drying process and therefore might require extensive experimentation.

If you make a real blunder, simply wash the entire surface clear with cellulose thinner and start again.

8 Both the game boards illustrated are mounted on pieces of wood which were slotted especially to hold the glass.

If you know of anyone who has access to a circular saw, this may be the answer for you, but I would suggest that you use hardwood or even black plastic extrusion which is shaped to form the runners for sliding doors. This is readily available from your wood supplier.

The fact that there are normally (but not always) two slots in such

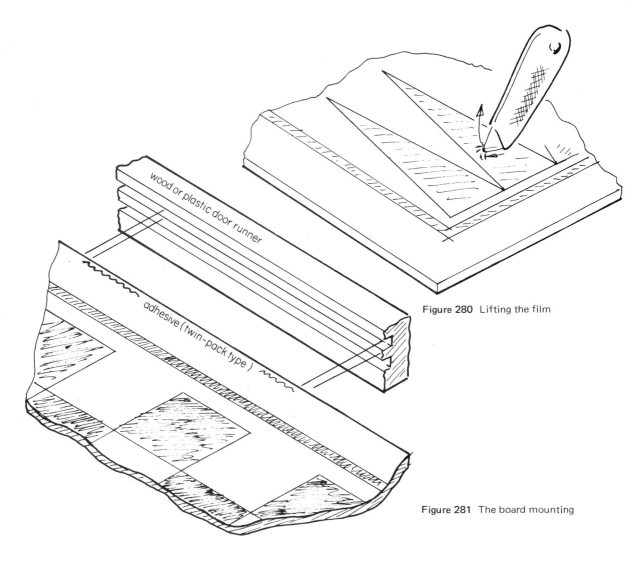

Figure 280 Lifting the film

wood or plastic door runner

adhesive (twin-pack type)

Figure 281 The board mounting

material is unimportant. Very few people will recognise it since its use in this context is totally unrelated to the use for which it was originally designed.

Cut the runner to the required length.

Smooth the ends with fine glass or garnet paper.

Glue the glass into the slot (Figure 281) using twin-pack adhesive.

Chessmen — Method

Natural, unstained wood is to my mind undoubtedly the best choice of material for chessmen. The choice, of course, is up to you, depending on what is available at your local suppliers. I would not, however, recommended pine, as the light-colour choice, but would go instead for light- and dark-coloured hardwood.

Every piece described here is made from 25 mm (1 in) section pieces of wood. The designs illustrated are only suggestions and, if you keep two points in mind, there is no reason why you should not design your own pieces. Firstly, chessmen should be distinct and recognisable from above — the normal position of viewing. Secondly, there is a great deal of duplication in the manufacture of most pieces — there are sixteen pawns, each of which should be identical. So *keep it simple.*

Do not cut all the individual lengths and then start work on the shaping as the small pieces of wood are too difficult to hold.

Working with an uncut length of wood, shape the head of each piece and *then* cut it from the main piece of wood, to the required length.

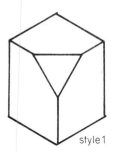
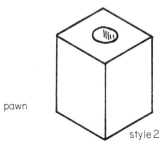

pawn

style 1   style 2

a

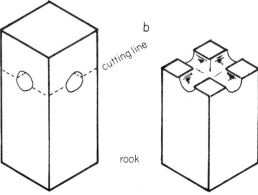

b

cutting line

rook

Pawn (height 35 mm (1½ in))
Two designs are shown in Figure 282. Both are extremely simple.

In style 1, a corner is surformed off, and in style 2 a 9 mm (⅜ in) hole is drilled into the centre for about 10 mm (½ in). To find the centre, draw diagonals on the end of the wood.

Figure 282 *Above, below and overleaf*
Some designs for pawn, rook, knight, bishop, queen and king

Rook (height 45 mm (2 in))
To give this piece the traditional turret appearance, two 9 mm (⅜ in) holes are drilled at right angles to each other at the same level. The wood is subsequently cut through the holes to give the desired effect (Figure 282).

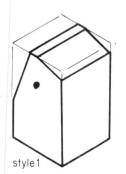

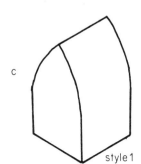
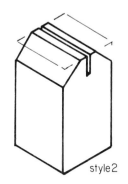

knight

c

bishop

style 1   style 2   style 1   style 2

Knight (height 45 mm (2 in))
How do you represent a horse in two easy cuts? Style 1 simplifies to the extreme the back of the neck and the nose. A 3 mm (⅛ in) hole is drilled as an eye (Figure 282).

Style 2 has only two ears and the neck line (Figure 282c). Is this enough?

Bishop (height 45 mm (2 in))
Two features of a bishop's mitred hat dominate these designs (Figure 282).

Style 1 shows the mitre shape alone. Style 2 the split in the centre of the mitre. Both pieces could be easily recognised from above.

queen

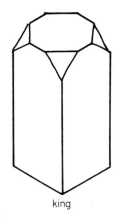
king

Queen (height 55 mm ($2\frac{1}{2}$ in))
The medieval type of aristocratic headwear is the theme behind this shape (Figure 282).

As for the rook, the 9 mm ($\frac{3}{8}$ in) diameter hole should be drilled and subsequently halved by sawing the top piece off.

King (height 60 mm ($2\frac{3}{4}$ in))
It is intended that the shape be reminiscent of a cut diamond or ruby (Figure 282). The edges should therefore be kept sharp.

GLOSSARY

Beading Hardwood strip having a constant cross-section; normally used to enhance the appearance or strength of edges or corners (Figure 283).

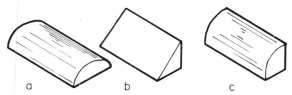

Figure 283 Three types of hardwood beading: (a) half round; (b) triangular (fillet); (c) quarter-round

Bench hook A device which enables wood to be firmly and safely held while sawing (*see* Tools, page 11).

Blind hole A hole which does not pass right through the material in which it is drilled.

Brad *see* Nails

Brassed Describes steel having a coating of brass to enhance its appearance, rather than corrosion-resistance properties.

Chamfered Describes a corner having its sharp edge removed by plane, Surform, or abrasive paper (Figure 284).

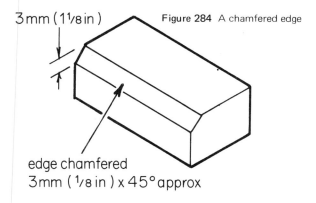

3mm (1⅛ in) Figure 284 A chamfered edge

edge chamfered
3mm (⅛ in) x 45° approx

Chipboard A man-made board, made from wood chips. Its normal thicknesses are 9 mm ($\frac{3}{8}$ in), 12 mm ($\frac{1}{2}$ in), 18 mm ($\frac{3}{4}$ in) and 25 mm (1 in).

Chuck The device on a drill which grips the drill bit.

Chuck Key A device which tightens the chuck jaws on the drill bit (normally only used on power drills).

Claw The part of the head of a carpenter's hammer, used for nail extraction.

Clearance hole A screw hole, the size of which equals the shank diameter of a screw. *See* table on page 17.

Clench To bend the protruding point of a nail over (in the direction of the grain) until it is flush with the surface.

Countersink A drilled recess which allows the head of a countersunk screw (*see* **Screw**) to be screwed flush with the surface.

Cramp A device for holding two pieces of material together until a glued joint sets (Figure 285).
See also Tools: cramp, page 12.

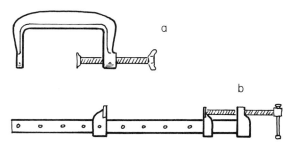

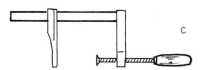

Figure 285 Three types of cramp: (a) 'G' cramp; (b) sash cramp; (c) 'quick release' cramp;

Cup washer *see* Screw cup.

Diameter When used in reference to a drill bit, this means the total thickness or width of the drill.

Dowel A length of round section material. It can be either wood or metal, but carpenters invariably use this word to refer to wooden dowel. It can be purchased in most common diameters up to 25 mm (1 in).

Dressed Planed to remove saw marks. When buying timber in inch sizes, the given or 'nominal' size refers to the sawn size. The planed size is about 3 mm ($\frac{1}{8}$ in) smaller, e.g. 1 in nominal approximately equals $\frac{7}{8}$ in dressed size.

End grain The rough part of a plank which shows the bow-shaped growth rings. It is difficult to obtain a good surface finish or to successfully drive screw nails into end grain.

Fillet A triangular section corner piece in either hardwood or softwood which can be either rough sawn or dressed (Figure 283b).

Flush Two contacting surfaces are said to be flush if there is no noticeable step along the line where they meet (Figure 86a).

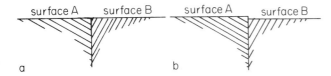

surface A   surface B   surface A   surface B

a   b

Figure 286 In (a), the two surfaces are 'flush'; in (b) they are not

Garnet paper A good quality abrasive paper.

Glass paper An abrasive paper, which is cheaper than garnet paper, but has a shorter useful life.

Glue block A piece of wood glued into a corner to increase the strength of a joint (Figure 287).

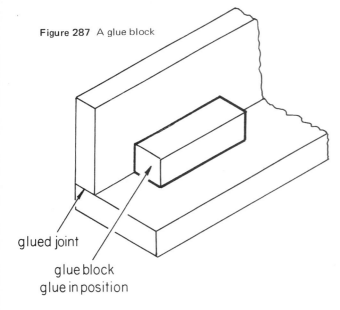

Figure 287 A glue block

glued joint

glue block
glue in position

Grain The direction along which the natural fibres lie in a plank of wood.

Growth rings The rings formed on a tree cross-section as it thickens season by season.

Hardboard A fairly cheap, thin, man-made board. It has one smooth side, the other having the texture of very rough sackcloth.

Hardwood The wood from a deciduous tree (leaves fall off in winter), e.g. mahogany, teak, sycamore, ramin, etc.

Jig-saw A portable saw specifically used for cutting curves in pieces of timber up to about 40 mm ($1\frac{1}{2}$ in) thick.

Joint A method of fixing two pieces of timber together by shaping the wood in question to create some interlocking pattern and by gluing.

Kerf The width of the groove made by a saw when it is cutting. If the kerf is not substantially wider than the saw blade material, the saw will jam as you are using it. You can rectify this fault in most carpenter's saws by having your tool dealer re-set the teeth.

Key A surface roughness which allows glue or paint to adhere firmly (see Glues and gluing, page 20).

Laying off The operation on the final coat of paint or varnish which involves brushing in one direction only (see Finishing, page 21).

Mitre A method of joining a corner using 45° cuts. This has the advantage of concealing the end grain (Figure 288).

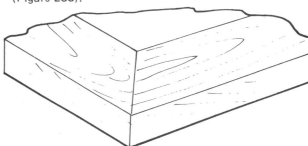

Figure 288 Detail of a table corner showing a mitred edge

Nail A metal pin for joining timber. Three basic types are shown in Figure 289a–c.

Round wire nail: sizes 25 mm (1 in) to 150 mm (6 in) — a general-purpose nail (Figure 289a)

Oval brad: sizes 18 mm ($\frac{3}{4}$ in) to 100 mm (4 in) — the flattened section helps to prevent grain splitting (Figure 289b).

Panel pin: sizes 12 mm ($\frac{1}{2}$ in) to 50 mm (2 in) — almost always used in conjunction with glue for fine work (Figure 289c).

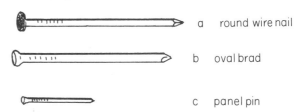

a   round wire nail

b   oval brad

c   panel pin

Figure 289 Three popular nail types

Nail punch A device used to sink a snail head below the surface (see Nailing, page 15).

Nominal see dressed

Orbital sander A popular sanding attachment for portable power drills.

Particle board (USA) a board made by binding small particles of wood together (*see* **Chipboard**).

Pilot hole A screw hole approximately $\frac{1}{2}$ to $\frac{3}{4}$ the shank diameter of a screw. The thread of the screw should get a good grip when driven into such a hole (*see* Table on page 17).

Plywood A man-made board consisting of three or more veneers glued together with the grains running at right angles to each other. Available in thicknesses from 1 mm ($\frac{1}{32}$ in) to 25 mm (1 in). If you intend to use plywood in an outdoor environment be sure to use an exterior or marine grade.

Proud One edge is said to be proud of another if it is the higher of the two (Figure 286b).

Rubbed joint A joint formed between two glued surfaces when all air has been expelled from the joint by squee-geeing (*see* Glues and gluing, page 19).

Sanding block An easily-held block of wood or cork around which abrasive paper can be wrapped (*see* Tools, page 11).

Sand paper The common name for glass or garnet abrasive paper.

Screw A threaded fixing (Figure 290) defined by the following features: length; shank thickness (No. 4, 6, 8, 10 — the shank becomes thicker as the number increases); type of head; and material (steel, brass, stainless steel).

Screw cup A type of washer used with countersunk screws either for appearance or to remove the need for countersinking the clearance hole.

Sectioned view A 'cut-away' view of an object drawn so as to reveal internal detail.

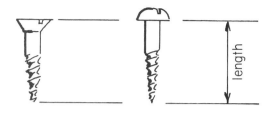

countersunk head   round head

Figure 290 Screw nails

Shank The unthreaded portion of a screw.

Softwood Wood coming from a coniferous tree, e.g. red pine, sitka spruce, and douglas fir.

Spoke-shave A special two-handed plane used for shaping curves.

Stripped The wood fibres which grip the screw thread can be torn away (or stripped) by over-tightening the screw. The gripping power of such a screw is then greatly diminished.

Template A paper, card, or thin metal pattern, made for easy reproduction of the pattern.

Thread The 'screw' part of a screw nail.

Try-square An L-shaped tool, used for the accurate marking out or checking of a 90° angle.

Veneer A very thin sheet of wood (approximately 1 mm ($\frac{1}{32}$ in)) chosen for its attractive appearance. It is normally used as a covering for less attractive wood or board.

Wander A twist drill can sometimes move erratically or 'wander' over a surface before it bites and starts drilling. This makes it difficult to drill at any exact spot unless a small hole (formed with a nail tip) is made at the correct location before beginning to drill.

SUPPLIERS

The projects in this book have been devised to make use of easily available materials, but in case you have any difficulty getting hold of wheels and axles for the baby walker I list suppliers who will be able to help you:

UK
Hobby's
Knight's Hill Square
London
SE27 0HH

USA
Woodcraft Supply Corporation
313 Mountvale Avenue
Woburn
Massachusetts 01801
USA